Could It Be This
Simple
?

A BIBLICAL MODEL
FOR HEALING THE MIND

TIMOTHY R. JENNINGS, M.D.

Autumn
House® Publishing
www.autumnhousepublishing.com

Published by Autumn House® Publishing, a division of Review and Herald® Publishing, Hagerstown, MD 21741-1119

Autumn House® titles may be purchased in bulk for educational, business, fund-raising, or sales promotional use. For information, please e-mail SpecialMarkets@reviewandherald.com.

Autumn House® Publishing publishes biblically based materials for spiritual, physical, and mental growth and Christian discipleship.

The author assumes full responsibility for the accuracy of all facts and quotations as cited in this book.

Unless otherwise noted, Bible texts are from the *Holy Bible, New International Version.* Copyright © 1973, 1978, 1984, International Bible Society. Used by permission of Zondervan Bible Publishers.

Texts credited to NEB are from *The New English Bible.* © The Delegates of the Oxford University Press and the Syndics of the Cambridge University Press 1961, 1970. Reprinted by permission.

Texts credited to NKJV are from the New King James Version. Copyright © 1979, 1980, 1982 by Thomas Nelson, Inc. Used by permission. All rights reserved.

Bible texts credited to NRSV are from the New Revised Standard Version of the Bible, copyright © 1989 by the Division of Christian Education of the National Council of the Churches of Christ in the U.S.A. Used by permission.

Texts credited to Tanakh are from *Tanakh: A New Translation of the Holy Scriptures According to the Traditional Hebrew Texts.* © The Jewish Publication Society of America, Philadelphia, 1985.

This book was
Edited by Gerald Wheeler
Copyedited by James Cavil
Designed by Trent Truman
Cover photo by iStockphoto
Typeset: Bembo 11/13

PRINTED IN U.S.A.

12 11 10 09 08   7 6 5 4 3

Library of Congress Cataloging-in-Publication Data

Jennings, Timothy R., 1961-   .
  Could it be this simple? : a biblical model for healing the mind / Timothy R. Jennings.
     p. cm.
  ISBN 978-0-8127-0435-8
  1. Mental health—Religious aspects—Christianity. 2. Spiritual healing. 3. Spiritual warfare. I. Title.
  BT732.4.J46 2008
  234'.131—dc22

                                        2006035266

DEDICATION

For Her

ACKNOWLEDGMENTS

I t would not have been possible to bring you this book without the patient, understanding, and loving support of my wife, Christie. Christie, you have shown me again and again God's graciousness, goodness, and love. Through you He has touched my soul. Thank you! I love you!

I also want to acknowledge my mother and the many friends who have prodded, encouraged, and supported me through the process of writing.

Most important, I want to thank God, who has graciously given me the opportunity to prepare this book.

∞

All patient accounts described in this book are true. I have changed all names and identifying information to protect confidentiality. Some of the cases presented combine information from multiple individuals so as to protect confidentiality further.

CONTENTS

Preface 7

CHAPTER 1 The Power of Belief 9

CHAPTER 2 The Hierarchy of the Mind 17

CHAPTER 3 The Destroyer Within 29

CHAPTER 4 The Balance Upset 37

CHAPTER 5 The Law of Liberty 44

CHAPTER 6 Shadow People 51

CHAPTER 7 The Law of Love 59

CHAPTER 8 Love's Counterfeits 67

CHAPTER 9 Faith—Fact or Fiction? 78

CHAPTER 10 Restoring Order 86

CHAPTER 11 Spiritual Warfare 97

CHAPTER 12 Forgiveness 110

CHAPTER 13 THE Casualties of War 121

CHAPTER 14 The Way of Death 135

CHAPTER 15 Coming Out of the Shadows 150

CHAPTER 16 The Mind Restored 155

PREFACE

She thought Her* life was worthless—no good for anything or anyone. Little did She realize how Her life was about to touch mine. My patient had no idea that she was about to send me on a journey, one lasting 13 years and leading to the writing of this book.

I was in my second year of psychiatric residency when I first met Her. The sky was gray and drizzly, yet I was hoping for a quiet day on call. I guess there was nothing wrong with hoping. I had just finished making avocado dip and was looking forward to an afternoon of watching football and munching on chips when the blare of my pager reminded me that I was a resident and that football would have to wait. Leaving the TV on and the chips on the table, I rushed to Eisenhower Army Medical Center (EAMC), located at Fort Gordon in Augusta, Georgia, for my first solo "psychiatric emergency."

When I first saw Her, She looked rather ordinary. How could I have ever known that Her story would affect me so? She seemed so sad, so lonely, so pitiful, and her face had a careworn appearance. Although She was only 47, Her skin was leathery, wrinkled, aged. Her hair was an unnatural shade of orange. Instead of makeup, Her cheeks showed the tracks of tearstains. She wore the traditional psychiatric hospital blue uniform.

A psychiatric attendant had been posted in the room to provide a 24-hour watch to prevent any further attempts at suicide. Although Her eyes appeared to focus on nothing in particular, I sensed something inside Her screaming for help. Having failed to complete Her most recent suicide attempt, She seemed to have lost hope and had succumbed to apathy and discouragement. And now she was my responsibility.

As I learned more about Her, I discovered a sad and painful history— the consequences of which She still struggled to resolve. She told me that She had grown up in Scotland in a conservative Christian home. Her parents had taught Her to respect Her parish priest as God's representative here on earth. But, She explained, the man had sexually molested Her from the ages of 6 to 10 and would afterward tell Her of Her sinfulness and need for repentance, lest She burn in the torments of hell.

Then She went on to describe Her life as a tumultuous history of one failed relationship after another. She had experienced chronic mood shifts, been haunted by nightmares and intrusive memories of the abuse, and suffered from anxiety, rage, and anger—especially when asked to trust someone.

Even more troubling, though, She struggled with a chronic fear of God, and was plagued with questions: "Did God do this to Me? Was it His will that I be abused? Does He hate Me? If God is love, why would He allow children to be abused? Or does He even exist?" So far in Her life, She had failed to find answers to quiet the storm in Her soul. She recounted how She had made various unsuccessful attempts to escape from the heartache. Drugs, alcohol, and sexual liaisons had left Her empty. When the pain became unbearable, She had attempted suicide.

Because I was still in residency, regulations required me to present all of my patients' cases to a staff psychiatrist for weekly supervision. When Her case came up in supervision, my faculty felt that the issues involved in it lay outside the realm of psychiatry, that She should be referred to a chaplain to address these issues. After I discussed the possibility with Her, She agreed to meet with a chaplain, but requested that it not be one of Her childhood faith.

After She had completed several visits with the EAMC chief of chaplains, I asked Her how the sessions were going. "Very strange," She said. "He told Me not to read my Bible. He told Me not to pray. Instead, he told Me to write a list of every bad and painful thing that has ever happened to me. Then he told Me to imagine a beam of light coming through the window and burning up the list. After that I was to tear up the paper, and My problems would be over." Of course the exercise did not eliminate Her problems, nor was she any closer to calming the tempest in Her soul or to finding answers to Her questions about God and His role in her life.

As I sat there listening, I felt so powerless. I wanted to help Her, to answer Her questions, to remove Her pain. But I didn't have the answers. All I could do was listen. I had nothing of substance to offer—and it angered me. It was then, at that moment, that I resolved to find answers—real ones that would bring real healing so I could offer something to help heal the pain. This book is a result of that search.

My patient thought Her life was worthless. She concluded that She didn't matter, that no one cared. But She was wrong. Her life did matter. It mattered to me. I am privileged to have known Her. And maybe, just maybe, many others will recognize how meaningful Her life really was.

---

* I have, as a way of indicating her impact on my life and career, capitalized pronouns when referring to this patient throughout this book.

CHAPTER 1

The Power of Belief

I could bore you with pages describing the turmoil of struggling to find meaningful answers from the many psychiatric texts. I could describe the theories of Freud, "the father of psychiatry," or Jung, Sullivan, Adler, Kernberg, Kohut, Beck, and so many more who followed. But as I read each of those theories something was missing, something didn't add up. As I tried to make sense of it all I realized that each of the theorists was describing a piece of a larger puzzle, a fragment of a greater whole, but even if you took everything they said, it still didn't all fit together.

Because so many of the theories took positions that conflicted with each other, it obscured any grand master design and made a cohesive understanding of the mind difficult to find. A unifying model of the mind was needed—one that ordinary people could understand. I knew that if I was going to help someone like the patient I described in the preface, the answers must be straightforward, sensible, and clear. Therefore I began with the basics and built from there.

Software and Hardware

The mind is an intricately complex bioelectric supercomputer. And just like the computers we buy in stores, the mind has both hardware and software. The term *hardware* refers to the actual physical components from which a computer is built (i.e., the hard drive, the video card, the network card, etc.). The hardware that forms our mental computer is the brain tissue itself. with all of its billions of neurons (nerve cells).

But hardware is not enough for a computer to function. It must also have software—or programming. A computer must have an "operating

9

system"—a framework of rules to direct its functioning. Microsoft Windows would be an example of such an operating system. The brain comes with hardware or hardwiring that has genetically programmed it with certain features that make it ready to receive an operating system.

The operating system gets installed/instilled during childhood and constantly undergoes modification throughout life. The language we speak, the God we worship, our beliefs, values, morals, how we play and interact with others—all are part of this complex operating system.

But hardware and software are still not enough for a computer to work. It must also have an energy source. If the energy source is faulty, glitches and short circuits can occur in the operation of the computer. The energy source for our brain is the blood that brings nutrients and takes away waste. If something interferes with reliable and consistent blood flow or if the blood itself is unhealthy, then the function of the brain suffers. Understanding this principle helps us recognize the benefits of a healthy lifestyle.

We all know that store-bought computers can have problems with hardware, or software, or both. The question hotly debated in psychiatry is whether mental illness results from hardware issues (genetic or structural brain problems) or software difficulties (problems in the operating system, i.e., in what or how we think) or both.

Further complicating this uncertainty is the entire field of religion and spirituality. What role do spiritual beliefs play in the functioning of the mind? Traditionally, psychiatrists have considered religious beliefs to be, at best, outdated coping strategies and, at worst, a mass delusion.

Such devaluing of religion was extremely personally frustrating because many of my professors persistently and subtly attacked my religious beliefs. They suggested that an enlightened individual would not need to cling to religious superstition. However, as a good scientist, I would not allow the criticism of others to close my mind to an arena of potential information without first investigating the evidence and drawing my own conclusion. Therefore, my residency became not only a time to study psychiatry, but also a time for deep introspection and investigation of my lifelong religious convictions.

I am extremely thankful to my professors for not allowing me simply to proclaim positions as true without supporting them with evidence and a well-thought-out rationale. Such an approach was the key to unifying the many contradictions in psychiatry, the key to understanding the mind. The more I studied psychiatry while simultaneously exploring the spiritual nature of human beings, the more clearly I could see a grand design that was beautiful and harmonious.

But despite the fact I was finding answers where traditional psychiatry feared to tread, most of my professors and many mental health professionals continue to hold the position that religious belief doesn't belong in the legitimate practice of psychiatry—that scientific understanding has eliminated the need for God.

Many cling to the position of Sigmund Freud, who described belief in God as a "societal neurosis" and called for intellectual understanding to remove the need for such a belief.[1] Others, who identify themselves as neuropsychiatrists, consider mental illness a result of chemical imbalance in the brain and contend that appropriate treatment is simply a matter of finding the proper combination of medications to restore normal brain chemistry. In other words, some health-care providers focus exclusively on the "hardware" while ignoring the "software."

Do Our Beliefs Matter?

With the above considerations in mind, I realized that the most reasonable next step in my journey was to seek the answers to several basic questions: Do our beliefs matter? Can they really affect us? Does our "software" actually make a difference? Or are we all merely genetically programmed (hardwired) to be the way we are? Can we, by changing what we think or the way we think, affect our physical and mental health? Thus I began to search for evidence to answer such complex questions.

While only a few psychiatrists have pursued the integration of spirituality with psychiatry, general medicine has developed a greater openness toward focusing on spiritual issues. As a part of this trend, Dr. Herbert Benson, of Harvard University, and his colleagues recently conducted a seminar designed to focus more attention on the importance of spirituality in medicine. The seminar leaders hold the position that a particular form of meditation results in overall physical benefit. More important, though, they emphasize that certain forms of spirituality actually improve physical health.

Cobra Venom for Chest Pain?

In his book *Timeless Healing: The Power and Biology of Belief* Dr. Benson documents in considerable detail the scientific data demonstrating that what we believe can significantly influence our physical health. Benson describes how he and his colleague Dr. David P. McCallie, Jr., documented an extensive list of various treatments designed to alleviate angina pectoris, the chest pain associated with decreased blood flow to the heart.

Their investigation discovered that, in the recent past, physicians have treated angina pectoris with unconventional methods (such as injecting cobra venom) and unnecessary surgeries (such as removing the thyroid or parts of the pancreas).

Although the medical community does not consider such methods as actually providing any physiological benefits, Drs. Benson and McCallie identified some extremely interesting results: such methods were effective for 70-90 percent of those patients who believed the intervention would work. When science eventually proved such treatments bogus, the rate dropped to 30-40 percent.[2]

Can Our Beliefs Prevent Nausea, Swelling, Rash, or Asthmatic Attack?

In his book Dr. Benson further addresses the effect of belief on physical health by referring to Dr. Stewart Wolf's investigation of intractable nausea during pregnancy. Wolf monitored stomach contractions by placing a bulb in the stomach of each expectant mother. The women were then given a medication identified as a cure for their nausea, while, in fact, they received syrup of ipecac—a substance that actually *causes* vomiting. Remarkably, all of the women experienced entire remission of their nausea and vomiting, and their stomach contractions returned to a normal rate (as measured by the bulb).[3]

Dr. Benson cites another study that examined the swelling that occurs in the aftermath of wisdom teeth extraction. In two randomly selected groups of patients one group received no treatment, while the second group received a mock treatment identified as helping to reduce the swelling. The mock treatment group experienced 35 percent less swelling than did the one receiving no treatment.[4]

Surprising results appeared in yet another study, one involving Japanese boys who had marked allergic reactions to the lacquer tree—a plant similar to poison ivy. After the researchers had blindfolded each boy, they brushed one arm with a branch from the lacquer tree, and the other arm with a chestnut branch. The researchers intentionally informed the boys that the lacquer branch was actually the chestnut branch, and that the chestnut branch was the lacquer.

Within minutes, patches of red bumps appeared, accompanied by itching and burning, on the arm that each boy had thought had been touched with the lacquer tree branch, but was actually stroked with the chestnut. The other arm had no reaction. The scientists determined that the reaction depended on genetic vulnerability to the toxin, the amount of toxin present, and the effect of suggestion. Most important, the re⸱ cluded that in 51 percent of the cases, the effect of sugge⸱ powerful than the other factors.[5]

A University of London study by N. R. Butler and Andrew Steptoe had asthmatics inhale what the researchers called a bronchoconstrictor, resulting in impaired breathing for 100 percent of the patients. But it did not affect those first treated with what they had been told was a powerful bronchodilator. In all cases the patients actually received sterile water.[6]

These and many similar experiments demonstrate that the mind exerts an overwhelming power over the body, and that what we believe can result in physical ailments or cures. The "software" does affect the "hardware." What we think actually has a powerful impact on our physical bodies.

Dr. Benson's research focused on how a patient's beliefs physically influence the body. But his investigations did not explore the effects that our beliefs have on the mind itself. As a result, a pair of questions inevitably arises: Do our beliefs affect our mental health? More important, do spiritual beliefs alter mental health?

Spiritual Issues Do Matter!

Numerous experiences have convinced me of the important role that spiritual beliefs play in our overall mental health. One of the most vivid and moving occurred during my service as division psychiatrist for the 3rd Infantry Division (Mechanized), stationed at Fort Stewart, Georgia.

During the fall of 1990 the United States and several of its allies had been gathering forces in the Middle East to prepare for an inevitable response to the invasion of Kuwait by Saddam Hussein's Iraqi forces. By February 1991 the anticipated assault on Iraqi forces in Kuwait seemed imminent.

Because military experts were convinced that Iraq would employ its arsenal of chemical and biological weapons, they had predicted as many as 80,000 U.S. casualties during the campaign. President George Bush had issued a deadline for Iraq to withdraw from Kuwait, and as the hours for invasion drew near, the tension increased.

As a commander of an M1A1 Abrams battle tank, Sergeant Jones managed one of the most powerful military vehicles in the world and was assigned to one of the armored divisions preparing to invade Iraq. While his military skills had earned him a large measure of respect among his colleagues, his strong Christian beliefs had also provided him a reputation throughout his entire battalion as a person of God.

With final preparations for invasion under way, Sergeant Jones asked his battalion chaplain for a container of sacred oil to anoint his tank. Using the oil, Sergeant Jones made a series of small crosses around the entire perimeter of the vehicle's hull, and dedicated himself, his men, and his tank to God. Among his prayers he asked that God not only protect him and his men in the approaching battle, but that He would also use him in a mighty way.

Shortly thereafter, Jones' company commander discovered that his radio was no longer operational. Because it was absolutely necessary that the company commander have a fully functional radio—to receive orders from battalion command, as well as to direct the rest of the units in his company—he ordered Sergeant Jones to give up his radio. Realizing that he would be essentially deaf on the battlefield and far more vulnerable, Jones attempted to refuse this order. Threatened with arrest and court-martial, he reluctantly surrendered his radio to his company commander.

Further complications arose when, after darkness fell and the soldiers mounted their vehicles to begin the invasion, Sergeant Jones discovered that his night vision equipment had ceased to operate. Alarmed that he and his tank comrades would be deaf and blind on the battlefield, Sergeant Jones promptly requested permission to withdraw. His superiors denied it. Although Sergeant Jones's tank could no longer fire with accuracy, as he would be unable to distinguish friend from foe, he could still draw enemy fire away from those tanks that still could locate targets.

Almost immediately after the invasion began, Sergeant Jones's company engaged the enemy and found themselves enveloped in fire from multiple sources: tank, mortar, artillery, and helicopter gunships. The night was ablaze with thunderous noise and exploding shells, vehicles, and the screams of injured men. Several units in Sergeant Jones's company received hits. His entire crew feared that death was imminent.

Four years after his service in Operation Desert Storm, Sergeant Jones visited my office seeking help with a variety of problems: nightmares, flashbacks, anxiety, sleep difficulty, relationship problems, tension, inability to concentrate, irritability, work problems, and depression. During the course of several sessions I became well acquainted with Sergeant Jones—what was important in his life, what motivated him to action, and how his Desert Storm experiences had affected him. His core conflict centered on the belief that God had let him down. By his fourth session I felt confident enough to present a series of statements that I believe summarized his Desert Storm experiences and that were essential to his overcoming the trauma of unresolved wartime experiences.

"You were a Christian. You made a public display of your Christianity. You put oil crosses all over your tank and dedicated yourself, your tank, and your men to God. You went into battle blind and deaf. And when your company came under attack, several other units were hit, but *not one bullet, shell, or piece of shrapnel damaged your tank.*"

After he had acknowledged each statement as true, I concluded, "Your Desert Storm experiences remind me of Daniel's experience in the lions' den."

The man's eyes opened wide, his jaw dropped, and the realization was immediate. With his head in his hands, he sat sobbing for several minutes. When he left my office that day, he took with him a new outlook on life.

Soon afterward, when I contacted him for follow-up, Jones informed me that his attitude toward life was so much improved that he saw no need for further sessions. Eighteen months later he on his own initiative shared with me his continued success. The nightmares and flashbacks had stopped, his sleep was normal, his anxiety and depression had remitted, and he had discontinued all medications. Having received an honorable discharge from the Army, he had completed his degree in education and had begun a new career teaching high school. His relationship with his wife was stronger than ever, and he was an active elder in his local church.

What had made the difference? Sergeant Jones had believed a lie. He had concluded that God had failed to answer his prayer, that the Lord had let him down. Now he realized the truth—that God had miraculously answered his prayer. It was the change in this belief that resulted in his recovery.[7]

Spiritual issues do matter! They are an integral part of our experience and must be included in our understanding and treatment practices.

---

[1] "Our knowledge of the historical worth of certain religious doctrines increases our respect for them, but does not invalidate our proposal that they should cease to be put forward as the reasons for the precepts of civilization. On the contrary! Those historical residues have helped us to view religious teachings, as it were, as neurotic relics, and we may now argue that the time has probably come, as it does in an analytic treatment, for replacing the effects of repression by the results of the rational operation of the intellect" (Sigmund Freud, *The Future of an Illusion* [1927], chap. 8; reprinted in *Complete Works,* eds. James Strachey and Anna Freud [1961], vol. 21). "Two paragraphs earlier Freud referred to religion as 'the universal obsessional neurosis of humanity,' arising, 'like the obsessional neurosis of children, . . . out of the Oedipus complex,' though he never actually used the phrase—often quoted in anthologies— 'religion is comparable to a childhood neurosis'" (quoted from *The Columbia Dictionary of Quotations* [Columbia University Press, 1998]).

[2] Herbert Benson, *Timeless Healing: The Power and Biology of Belief* (New York: Scribner, 1996), p. 30.

[3] *Ibid.,* p. 32.

[4] *Ibid.*, p. 33.
[5] *Ibid.*, p. 59.
[6] *Ibid.*, p. 54.
[7] Medications do not change beliefs. However, they can offer symptom relief. Delusions are by definition fixed false beliefs, and medications can result in change in those suffering from delusional beliefs. How does this happen if the medications themselves don't alter beliefs? People suffering with delusions have lost the ability to reason or perceive reality accurately. Medications work by restoring the person's capacity to reason or accurately perceive reality, and the person is then able to evaluate the facts and evidence and, by the use of their own reasoning power, to change their delusional beliefs to reality-based ones.

CHAPTER 2

The Hierarchy of the Mind

As I continued to see patients with symptoms similar to those exhibited by Her and Sergeant Jones, I became even more interested in finding a working model of the mind to offer real answers for ordinary people. Consequently I intensified my investigation of the mind, its faculties, and the spiritual nature of humanity. What I discovered was exciting and life-changing.

God is a deity of order. When He creates, He does not do so chaotically, but in an orderly, organized manner. When God made humanity, He designed their brains to function in a certain way. In this chapter we will explore the organizational structure of our mind. Understanding its hierarchy will enable us to make intelligent choices in its healing.

The Highest Faculties

The highest faculties we possess are those that most directly reflect the image of God, ones that many Christians refer to as our "spiritual nature" and that God intended to govern us. The spiritual nature is not an ethereal, mystical, vaporous entity that enters or leaves the body. It consists of those qualities and abilities that make us most Godlike, most in His image. They are the traits that separate us from the animals and make us accountable to God.

Spiritual Nature

Mind

The Ability to Reason

The highest faculty in our mind is the ability to *reason*—to think, to weigh evidence, and then to draw conclusions. It enables us to contemplate and to understand.

My neighbor's dog Daisy is a typical mutt, full of energy, often seeking to be petted, and always wanting to please. Daisy has a problem, though. She frequently goes through the neighborhood picking up whatever she can find—sticks, trash, old shoes—and drops it on my neighbor's porch.

If my neighbor happens to be in his yard when the dog comes home with her latest treasure, she drops her prize at his feet and looks up with her big brown eyes, wagging her tail, wanting to be petted. Daisy doesn't understand that what she has done does not please my neighbor, but is rather a nuisance. My neighbor cannot explain this to her. Animals cannot reason.

Humans, on the other hand, do possess the ability to reason, and it is the highest of all mental faculties.

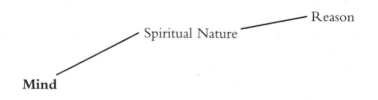

God Designed the Conscience

But because humans don't possess infinite knowledge, reason alone is not sufficient for healthy decision-making or discrimination. As a further aid, therefore, God designed the *conscience* to work jointly with reason.

The conscience is the spiritual eye (see Matt. 6:22). It is the faculty through which the Spirit of God communicates directly to us, the one that "hears" the voice of God speaking quietly (see 1 Kings 19:12). When some Christians say, "The Spirit told me in my spirit," they are referring to their conscience. It's healthy for us to remember, though, that just as our physical eye can be diseased, so can the conscience.

A dermatologist friend holds a weekly Bible study in his office. Just prior to the start of one 6:00 p.m. meeting, Joe, one of the members of his group, arrived for the Bible study without his wife. He explained that their 15-year-old blind and deaf dog was lost. His wife had stayed home to search for the dog, and Joe had come to the Bible study to ask members of the group to pray that they would soon find the animal safe.

After the group had prayed, Joe left to rejoin the search for the pet. Within a short while—at approximately 6:30 p.m.—Jeremy, another member of the group, interrupted the Bible study to say that he had just been impressed with a vision of Joe's dog in the woods, and that Joe had located it. Jeremy told the group that their prayers had been answered—that the animal was safe. Amazingly, at 7:00 p.m., Joe called to report that he and his wife had located their pet in the woods behind their house exactly at 6:30 p.m. How did Jeremy know?

God can speak directly to the mind, either audibly or via impressions. The avenue by which we hear His communications to us would be either our auditory neurons, if the voice is audible, or the conscience, if it is a mental impression.

The conscience is a specific mental faculty sometimes referred to as the spiritual eye. Just as the physical eye can turn light into neural energy and transmit information to the brain, the conscience transmits spiritual impressions to the brain for understanding. Remember that the physical eye can be diseased and unhealthy and therefore see things unclearly or even things that do not really exist. In a similar manner, the conscience can become diseased and unhealthy, causing people to experience impressions that are distorted or even totally fanciful.

Initially, information reaching the mind via the conscience *has no greater value than information reaching us through any other avenue.* Our reasoning powers must evaluate it to determine if the impression or voice is, in fact, from God, or a counterfeit. Therefore, we may be impressed with some message or idea, but that impression or idea is not evidence in itself. It will have validity only as corroborating evidence supports it.

God designed reason and conscience to work in concert with one another for healthy discernment and discrimination as well as for valid decision-making. When reason functions alone without conscience, one may develop very intellectual theories (such as evolutionism or Marxism) that may have the appearance of wisdom but deny the existence of God and the principles of His government.

Reason working without conscience can also rationalize unhealthy behavior in order to avoid responsibility and corrective action. Many criminals use their reasoning abilities to commit crimes and to evade capture, but that can occur only when the conscience is unhealthy or inactive. To make healthy choices, reason must have the restraining hand of conscience.

Mohandas K. Gandhi, Indian political and spiritual leader, stated that "attribution of omnipotence to reason is as bad a piece of idolatry as is worship of stock and stone believing it to be God. I plead not for the suppression of reason, but for a due recognition of that in us which sanctifies reason."[1]

It is the influence of God working through the conscience and via the revelation of truth that sanctifies (makes healthy) the reason. Conscience alone, however, cannot be trusted to guide without the balance of reason. When conscience leads our decision-making independently from reason, one may end up burning in Waco, drinking cyanide in Jonestown, trying to ride the Hale-Bopp comet, or flying airplanes into buildings. After all, to burn to death with David Koresh and the Branch Davidians, to commit mass suicide with Jim Jones or the Heaven's Gate cult, or to turn passenger planes into suicide bombs, one may be conscientious—but what about reasonable?

German philosopher Friedrich Nietzsche stated:

"Again and again I am brought up against it, and again and again I resist it: I don't want to believe it, even though it is almost palpable: the vast majority lack an intellectual conscience; indeed, it often seems to me that to demand such a thing is to be in the most populous cities as solitary as in the desert."[2]

The Tragedy of an Unreasonable Conscience

Recently I experienced a tragic reminder of the damage that can occur when conscience operates without the balance of reason. Carlos was a 69-year-old retired professor who belonged to a conservative Christian denomination. He had recently retired following a fulfilling 35-year career teaching history at a private college.

Living an extremely conservative lifestyle, he strictly adhered to many rigid rules. Carlos ate a vegetarian diet, avoided alcohol and tobacco, and exercised regularly. But Carlos and his wife also believed it was sinful to take medications—in particular, psychiatric medications. They believed such substances would damage the brain.

In the fall of 2000 Carlos became severely depressed. Losing touch with reality and beginning to hear voices, he became paranoid and believed that others were watching him. Eventually he lost the ability to interact appropriately with those around him. Carlos and his wife didn't know what to do. Clearly he was ill, but they had no idea how to treat him without medication.

Desperate, they searched for help until they found a remote institution staffed by physicians who shared their belief that psychiatric medications

20

would damage his brain. Because of their belief, they treated him with "natural remedies"—herbs, hydrotherapy, and prayer.

Unfortunately Carlos continued to regress, and soon he was incoherent, crawling around on the floor. Incontinent of bowel and bladder, he would smear feces on the walls. He was inconsolable, agitated, and grossly psychotic. Because he was no longer eating, his weight plummeted until he was starving to death.

When Carlos reached 83 pounds (he's five feet nine), the physicians at the institution had a feeding tube inserted through his abdominal wall directly into his stomach, and they began to feed him manually. While his weight improved slightly, his depression, paranoia, and irrational thinking persisted. Eight months of such "treatment" produced no improvement, and in absolute desperation his wife brought Carlos to my office.

The man was in a pitiful state. The skin hung loosely from his cheeks, and his eyes had sunk deeply into their sockets with dark rings circling the orbits. It was painful for Carlos to sit—his bones were almost protruding through his skin. He was severely depressed and continued to be psychotic. His wife, however, insisted that her husband receive absolutely no medications even if it led to his death.

For more than an hour I sought to reason with the couple, explaining the scientific evidence that psychosis is actually damaging to the brain, and that the longer one remains psychotic, the more difficult it is to treat successfully. I reviewed the history of Carlos's failure to respond to "natural remedies" and the history of "natural remedies" failing to improve mental illness during the nineteenth century.

My attempt to direct them away from "natural remedies" led me to mention the molecular activity of the new medications and their specific effects on the brain. I informed Carlos and his wife of both the expected benefits and the potential side effects. They would not budge.

In yet another attempt I asked them to look at Carlos to see what eight months of "natural remedies" had accomplished. He was nearly dead. In their minds, however, they considered it better to let him die than to treat him with medications, even if the medications would restore his health. The situation was heartbreaking. The couple conscientiously sought to do what they thought was right, *but by failing to use their* reasoning *powers, their choices actually resulted in greater harm.*[3]

It is only when reason and conscience work together, in harmony and balancing one another, that healthy decision-making can occur. Together the faculties of reason and conscience comprise what we know also as our judgment. Dysfunction of either reason or conscience results in impaired judgment, while the healthier our reason and conscience become, the better our judgment.

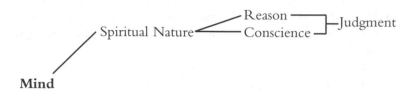

Everyone Worships Something

The final faculty that completes our spiritual nature is an innate desire or drive to worship. An inherent part of our being, it is experienced by everyone, whether they admit it or not. It might not be God, but it could be the Dallas Cowboys, money, power, a pop culture figure such as Madonna, the scientific method, or oneself. But everyone worships something. Some might call this a drive for meaning or purpose—a looking outside of oneself for a frame of orientation, for something that gives focus, meaning, purpose, and understanding to life.

In his book *Way to Wisdom* Karl Jasper summarizes the situation this way: "That which you hold to, upon which you stake your existence, that is truly your God."[4] Richard Creel offers similar insight in *Religion and Doubt:* "A person's deity is that which actually dominates that person's life, giving it unity, direction, and inspiration, whether the person realizes it or not."[5]

The question is not Do we worship? but rather What are we worshipping?

By Beholding We Become Changed

Christianity teaches us to look not at self but at Christ. Why does God say, "Worship Me"? Is He insecure? Does He somehow need our validation and approval? Does it really matter what we worship?

God tells us to "worship Me" because we actually adapt ourselves to the things we admire and devote ourselves to the things we idealize. Psychiatry calls it modeling, and in the Bible it is the law of worship: by beholding, we become changed. Our character actually becomes transformed to reflect that which we revere (2 Cor. 3:18).

Among the many gods that the ancient Egyptians worshiped was a frog. Imagine your family gathered in the evening for worship around the idol of a little golden frog. "Dear lord frog . . ." Would this help the mind to grow and expand in attaining higher levels of development?

We need not turn to ancient Egypt to discover startling examples of worship. For example, we can visit modern India to find a sect of Hinduism that worships the rat. It maintains temples dedicated to honoring the rat. The temples contain large idols of rats, and, not surprisingly, real rats infest the temples themselves.

As part of their worship, sect members bring grain to feed the rats that infest the temples. While we might prefer to avoid risking contact with the creatures, this sect considers it a great blessing to be bitten by a rat. So strong is their dedication that members of the sect pray that when they die they might be reincarnated as a rat. Think about it: beings created in the image of God with individuality, the power to think and to act (Ps. 115:5-8; Rom. 1:21-32), who now have as their highest goal to become a rat.

Why does God ask us to worship Him? He does so because He is the only one we can worship that will not cause us to degenerate. We, as humans, are the highest created beings on our planet. Therefore, our planet contains nothing that we can worship and that will advance us. To worship anything on it will merely lead to our own degradation.

Therefore, the choice of what or whom one worships greatly influences the development of the mental faculties. Because the god one serves directly affects the functioning of both reason and conscience, it is essential to practice healthy forms of worship. Healthy worship ennobles and strengthens our reason and conscience, while unhealthy forms of worship dwarfs and enfeebles them.

Our spiritual nature, therefore, is composed of reason, conscience, and worship—the highest faculties in our mind. Our spiritual nature is to direct the functioning of all the other aspects of our mind.

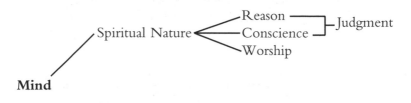

Mind / Spiritual Nature — Reason / Conscience / Worship — Judgment

The Will

God designed the next faculty of the mind—the *will*—to function at the direction of reason and conscience. The action center of the mind (the governor or executive agent), it is the part of the mind that actually chooses. God's plan intends the mind to function with will under the direction of reason and conscience, but humans do not always follow this divinely intended hierarchy.

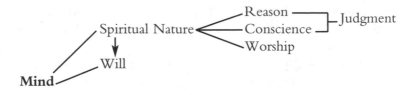

Consider the example of smokers who can list a variety of reasons that smoking is dangerous: increased risk of lung cancer, heart disease, stroke, and emphysema; the potential harm to their children's health; and the expense, odors, and inconvenience. Their conscience may convict them to quit smoking. They may even say to their friends, "I wish I'd never started smoking." But if they never engage their will and choose to put the cigarettes down and quit, they keep on smoking.

While God designed the will to operate at the direction of the spiritual nature, this is not always the case. When people exercise their will to choose to act in a manner that violates reason and conscience, they damage themselves, becoming restless, uneasy, and anxious. But when the will follows the direction of reason and conscience, then even though it might not feel good at the moment, healing occurs, and internal peace, confidence, and contentment result. We will explore this in more detail in later chapters.

The Thoughts

The next agency in the mind is the *thoughts,* which is subordinate to the spiritual nature and the will. While it includes all the mundane things we think each day, more specifically it involves our *beliefs, values, morals,* and *imagination.*

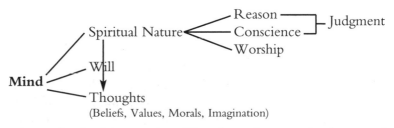

Some immediately object, stating, "I've always been taught that my values and morals govern my life and direct my actions. Shouldn't they be at the top?" I simply point out that reason can modify our beliefs, values, and morals, and the will can override them. Can those who do not believe in God, when presented new evidence and truth about God, reason through the new facts and change their beliefs? Certainly! And can a person exercise their will and choose to engage in activities that violate their own beliefs, values, and morals? Again, the answer is obvious. Imagination also is subject to the scrutiny and governance of reason, conscience, and will.

What I have described in the preceding paragraph is true for the mature—for those who have the ability to reason. But for children, and those whose ability to reason has not yet fully developed, beliefs enter the mind and get established in the mental operating system without a healthy evaluation of the basis for the belief. In fact, all of us reach adulthood with beliefs, values, and morals that need modification. As adults we have a responsibility to evaluate them for ourselves and keep all those that are healthy, all that are supported by the facts and truth, but discard or change all those that are remnants of a child's way of thinking. As Paul so eloquently stated: "When I was a child, I talked like a child, I thought like a child, I reasoned like a child. When I became a man, I put childish ways behind me" (1 Cor. 13:11).

Feelings

The final faculty of the mind, which in God's design is subordinate to all the others, is that of *feelings*. It includes the entire spectrum of emotions of which we are all familiar: sadness, joy, anger, happiness, and all the rest. But two particular types of feelings deserve special attention: a desire for relationships, and our affections.

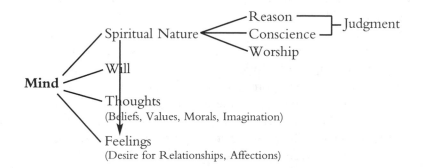

A Drive for Relationships

First, God has created us with an innate desire or *drive for relationships*. Everyone longs to be special, to love and be loved, to share and be shared with, to be in relationships. Such a desire for relationships is a biologically programmed part of our being. Our Creator made it part of our nature.

Some people object to this aspect of our mind being placed under feelings rather than included with our spiritual nature. They point out that God is a relational being, and contend that human beings, created in God's image, are also relational. Beginning with that premise, they conclude that we should include this aspect of our mind in our spiritual nature.

But it is important to recognize that all nature reveals something about God (Rom. 1:20), and, as all of us who have had pets understand, animals, in addition to humans, are also relational beings. Therefore, while demonstrating something about God, the desire for relationships does not distinguish us from the animals, so we should not consider it as part of our spiritual nature.

Rather, we should keep the desire for relationships subordinate to reason, conscience, and will, with these higher agencies evaluating the facts, circumstances, and evidences of a potential relationship and then permitting or rejecting its possibility. In fact, without the spiritual nature to govern the desire for relationships, human beings would become "like brute beasts, creatures of instinct" driven by passion and lust (2 Peter 2:12).

Our Affections

The second important feeling to identify is our *affections*. They are our emotional attachments, our heartstrings—the sentiments we develop for people and things.

Imagine that you have just purchased a new BMW. Eager to show it to your friends, you go to their place of employment. You rush in to get them, and when you come out you see a car identical to yours, except the other car has a noticeable dent in the front passenger door. How do you respond? Perhaps with a brief "That's too bad" and a quick return to the excitement of showing off your new wheels.

But what if, when you came out, it was your car with the big dent in the door? Would it feel different? This is an example of our affections, what the Bible refers to when it mentions guarding the heart. Be careful about what you become attached to. When Paul writes about circumcision of the heart by the Holy Spirit, he urges us to cut away unhealthy attachments and strengthen healthy attachments (Rom. 2:29).

The Original Harmony

God designed the mind to work in perfect balance, benefiting from face-to-face communion with Him. As Adam spent time with God he not only would make intelligent choices to follow God's will, but, via the law of worship, had every aspect of his mind permeated with the divine character. With God as the central focus, his mind was designed to operate with reason and conscience evaluating facts, circumstances, and evidence to determine what action, course, or conclusion was most appropriate. His will would then choose the course of action determined best by reason and conscience. It also would select what beliefs, values, and morals he would internalize and practice, how he used his imagination, what attachments he would make, how he would relate to God and others, and thus what character he would form. Unfortunately, Adam exercised his will to choose poorly, and we will explore the consequences of his choice in later chapters.

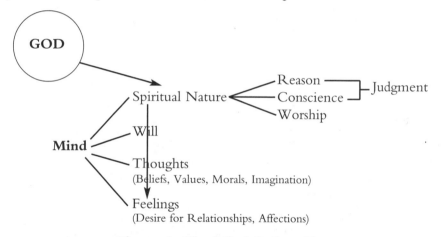

Figure 1. The Mind Before Sin

The model above diagrams the original faculties of the mind, their organizational hierarchy and interrelationship. Unfortunately, something has gone terribly wrong. Today, few human minds work with the divinely intended harmony. The mind is infected with a destructive element that interferes with a naturally harmonious and healthy mental function. In the next chapter we will discover the destructive element warping our minds, and begin to explore how to remove it.

[1] Mohandas Gandhi (1869-1948), in *Young India,* Oct. 14, 1924, quoted in *The Columbia Dictionary of Quotations.*

[2] Friedrich Nietzsche (1844-1900), *The Gay Science,* rev. ed. (1887), in *The Columbia Dictionary of Quotations.*

[3] Three years after Carlos left my office, the physician who referred him to see me told me the rest of the story. Carlos returned to the facility where he had been receiving his "natural remedy" treatments and continued that "treatment" without any improvement for another three months. Then Carlos's son, who lived outside the United States, discovered what was going on and immediately flew to the U.S. and took his father to a psychiatrist, who prescribed an antidepressant medication. Within six weeks Carlos's depression completely disappeared. His appetite became normal, he began gaining weight, his thoughts were clear and organized, and he was able to care for himself. After several months he even began teaching on a part-time basis.

[4] Karl Jasper, *Way to Wisdom* (New Haven, Conn.: Yale University Press, 1951).

[5] Richard Creel, *Religion and Doubt: Toward a Faith of Your Own* (Englewood Cliffs, N.J.: Prentice-Hall, Inc., 1977), p. 31.

CHAPTER 3

The Destroyer Within

Selfish persons are incapable of loving others, but they are not capable of loving themselves either.—Erich Fromm.

In the beginning God created the first human being (Adam) in His image. Originally humanity was perfect—genetically, mentally, and spiritually. Human beings possessed a pure conscience and noble reason, and experienced perfect worship in a face-to-face relationship with God, thus keeping all the other faculties of the mind in perpetual harmony and balance. The principles of love and liberty governed the mind. Peace and contentment were the constant outgrowth of a mind in perfect balance.

Unfortunately, such perfect balance did not last. Humanity broke its trust with God. By its own freewill choice, the human race severed its intimate connection to God. The consequences were devastating and immediate. As the harmonious balance of the mind destabilized, a destructive element replaced God's influence. A new principle now dominated the human mind.

Selfishness—self-seeking—displaced love and liberty. Human beings lost their innate sense of safety and security. Their experience of peace gone, they became consumed with fear and guilt, which led to a drive for self-preservation. Prior to Adam's selfish choice the human mind was free from fear. Fear was a new and devastating emotion that contaminated the human mind. It resulted from misjudgment of God and separation from Him. Because human beings no longer trusted the Lord for their welfare, the principle of survival of the fittest emerged.

Because Adam, without cause, chose to break trust with God and pursue his own self-interest, his conscience convicted him of guilt. This guilt, in turn, condemned Adam. Experiencing the condemnation of his own conscience, Adam was afraid for his life and so took matters into his own hands.

With his mind now consumed with fear and doubt, with love and liberty no longer the pervasive power in his heart, and with the principle of self-preservation firmly established, Adam set out to save himself. He ran and hid.

And humanity has been running and hiding from God ever since. Trust in God is gone, and selfishness now reigns supreme. The harmonious balance of the mind has shattered, and the destructive principle of selfishness now dominates its mental faculties. But for the grace of God the human race would be doomed.

Selfishness is the destructive element infecting the mind. It is not present in the mind as originally designed by God, but has become an infecting agent, an intruder, contaminating our mental faculties and destabilizing their function. Without God's intervention and plan to heal the mind, humanity's condition would be hopeless.

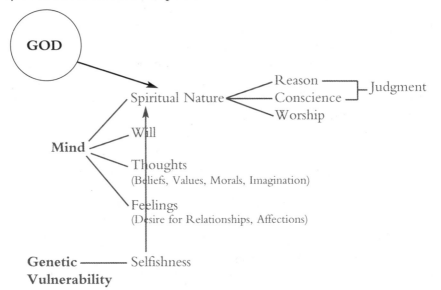

Figure 2. The Mind After Sin and Before Conversion

Born Self-centered

Psychiatrists recognize the selfish aspect of our being and refer to it as egocentrism. Not an acquired characteristic, it is innate. Because Adam broke trust with God and became self-centered, all humanity, as offspring of Adam, are born biologically and genetically self-centered. As David wrote in Psalm 51: "I was born with iniquity; with sin my mother conceived me" (verse 7, Tanakh).

How many infants are interested in whether Mother is well rested and fed? None. Babies focus on their own needs. It is our inheritance from Adam. When God created Adam, He delegated to him the ability to create beings in his image. Just as God created Adam in His own image, so after sin Adam produced children possessing his nature and qualities. This pattern continues today, as all parents have surely noticed.

Three Avenues of Selfishness

People express their biological predisposition toward self-centeredness in three main ways. The Kings James Version translation of 1 John 2:16 describes these tendencies as "the lust of the flesh, and the lust of the eyes, and the pride of life." In today's English we would simply say sensualism, materialism, and egotism. Each person has a different arrangement of the three traits, some with weaker or stronger aspects.

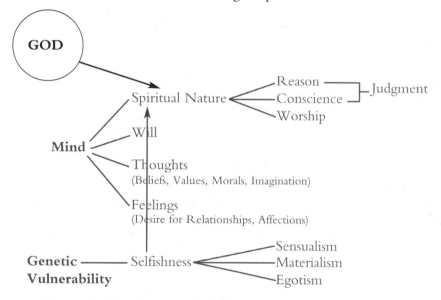

Figure 3. The Mind After Sin and Before Conversion

The Deceived Mind

If you are familiar with the concepts of Sigmund Freud, selfishness is the part of the mind he called the *id*. Freud considered the id a genetically programmed drive of sex and aggression that dominated our development. *Sensualism* is synonymous with what he labeled as sex, and relates to all forms of physical pleasure. While the category certainly involves sexual contact, it also includes drugs, alcohol, gluttony, and essentially all sensory pleasures.

Materialism is synonymous with greed, which consists of the pursuit of material possessions at the expense of others, and *egotism* involves putting self ahead of others. It's worth emphasizing that both *materialism* and *egotism* are aggressive behaviors.

Unless overcome, such primitive drives will lead to self-destruction. But because Freud did not acknowledge God's role in human life, he could not include Him in his treatment plan, so he chose the only logical alternative available to him: self.

Freud's theory states simply, "Where id is, ego shall be." As a result, Freudian theory of psychoanalysis involves the process of turning the mind's eye inward and attempting to bring the unconscious id into consciousness, where it can be controlled, modified, and changed. In other words, psychoanalysis is the process of focusing one's mind on selfish desires—the infectious, destructive element of the mind—with the belief that after such desires come into awareness, a person can make healthy changes.

A Christian model of treatment adds additional insights. Jeremiah 17:9 informs us that the human mind is "deceitful above all things, and desperately wicked; who can know it?" (NKJV). We must turn to God for His help. Otherwise, attempts to understand one's mind unaided by divine guidance can ultimately lead to further self-deception.

Another important factor in the treatment process is the law of worship, also known as modeling. Because of it we become like whatever we admire or worship. Whatever we idealize, whether it be a person, God, idea, or idol, we become more like it. We adapt ourselves to whatever we focus on. If we focus on self, we become more self-centered. As we train the mind to focus on the destructive, infecting element in our mind, its dangerous power strengthens.

This change occurs both in character and biology. The brain will actually rewire itself based on the things we think, do, see, and experience. Indeed, the brain is constantly branching and pruning its neural network. The choices we make—what we think, believe, admire, and worship, as well as the behavior in which we engage—all have profound effects on the ultimate development of our neural network and thus our characters. The software (what we think) can actually change the hardware (the neural network).

Perhaps some of you took Spanish or some other language in high school. If so, remember the difficulty you encountered in those first few weeks, learning one word at a time, agonizing as you tried to recall and pronounce that one word? As you studied and practiced, and your vocabulary increased, eventually even pronunciation and syntax improved. It occurred as the brain increased its neural network, the number of cells and cell-to-cell connections necessary for speaking the new language.

But if you've stopped speaking Spanish since graduating high school, what has happened to your proficiency? With continued use, the brain strengthens and expands the neural network. But when those pathways become idle, they eventually degrade and vanish. The same thing happens throughout the entire brain. This is why habits are not easily eliminated: the stronger a habit and the longer its existence, the more time and effort necessary for the pathways to disappear.

Now, you might be saying, "This is all very interesting, but what role does it have in healing the mind?" It is important because we have the power, by use of the will, to choose which neural circuits receive continued use in our brains. By the choices we make, we can cooperate with God for the actual transformation of our characters here and now. When we choose, in cooperation with God, to behave in ways that reason and conscience have determined most healthy, we receive divine power to follow through on those decisions.

Consider the example of smokers. They can pray for deliverance all they want, but until they decide to set the cigarettes down, they will continue to smoke. However, when they discard the cigarettes and seek God's help, they receive divine power sufficient for the task. The divine power enables the smokers to tolerate the agony of withdrawal and to experience eventual freedom from their cravings. Thus, over time, their neural circuitry changes, and the pathways that correspond to the habit of smoking slowly degrade while neural circuits responsible for self-control strengthen.

In September 1999 *Nature* magazine published research that further supports the fact that our actions and choices actually result in physical changes in the brain itself.[1] Conducted by a collaboration of scientists from Yale, Harvard, and Northwestern, the study revealed that a person's use of cocaine causes a change in the brain that activates previously dormant genes.

It means that certain behaviors can actually cause genes, which are turned off, to switch on and begin exerting their influence on the individual. In the case of cocaine, it activates a gene that causes the production of certain proteins that produce increased cravings for more cocaine.

Television and the Law of Worship

B. S. Centerwall conducted research that powerfully demonstrates the law of worship (modeling). He published his results in the *Journal of the American Medical Association*.[2] In an effort to assess the effects of television programming on violence in society, Centerwall developed an elaborate study to evaluate violence in society before and after the introduction of television. Because he wanted a clear-cut indicator of violence, he focused on homicide rates in the United States.

To avoid objections that any increase in the murder rate might result from easy access to guns, he compared the U.S. rates to those in Canada, a similarly Westernized country, but with strict gun control. Finally he compared the information from these two nations with statistics derived from South Africa, which did not allow television until the 1970s. As an added precaution he counted only White-on-White murder in South Africa to rule out any chance of the Apartheid policies of racism affecting the outcome. What he discovered was startling.

After introduction of TV, homicide rates in U.S. increased by 93 percent from 1945 to 1974. During the same period, homicide rates in Canada increased 92 percent. But in South Africa, in which TV did not appear until the 1970s, the homicide rates decreased by 7 percent from 1945 to 1974. Astoundingly, after the introduction of television in 1975, the homicide rate increased 130 percent.

In April 2004 the professional journal *Pediatrics* published astounding research that revealed television watching by children increases their risk of developing attention deficit disorder. The amount of time a child watches television changes the brain![3]

This evidence, in conjunction with other research with similar findings, has led the American Academy of Pediatrics to recommend no television of any kind for a child under 2 years of age and strict limitations on older children. Clearly, what we watch, behold, admire, worship, and believe has significant impact on whom we become.

The Body's Effect on the Mind

The faculties of the mind function best when the body is healthy. The mind and body are not separate. We have already discussed the mind's effect on the body. But we must also remember that the body clearly affects the functioning of the mind. When physical sickness occurs, the mind becomes less efficient. For example, who would want to take final exams with the flu and a temperature of 103° F?

The Machinery of the Brain Can Be Defective

We cannot forget that as we talk about the mind, physical disorders will impair its functioning. Humanity's break with God has not only weakened the mind with selfishness, but also subjected the brain to disease and physical defect.

Alzheimer's disease and stroke—as well as schizophrenia and other disorders—affect the physical brain itself (the hardware), and subsequently impair the functioning of the mind. Sometimes restoring wellness requires biological interventions (to treat the hardware), but at other times social, psychological, or spiritual interventions are needed (to treat the software). That's what makes psychiatry so challenging and exciting.

As a psychiatrist I often utilize medicines to stabilize a person's biochemistry. Medications can minimize the impact of genetic or environmental defects in the brain. Some of my Christian patients have difficulty with this and even experience guilt when taking psychiatric medications. A number have endured criticism from well-meaning friends.

I remind my patients that when Adam fell from grace, genetic defects began to enter our DNA. As a race we became subject to disease and death. Thus our brains do not operate as efficiently as Adam's did when he came directly from the hand of God. Our brains can, and often do, have various defects in the actual molecular structure and functioning of the cells. The hardware of our mental computer is occasionally defective, and medicines can sometimes improve the functioning of the mental hardware.

A recent discovery published in the *American Journal of Psychiatry* strikingly illustrates this.[4] Dr. Michael Egan and associates discovered that a single random gene mutation on chromosome 22 alters memory function.[5] Medications can compensate for a biological weakness, reduce the intensity of the unhealthy feelings, and improve brain efficiency, thus making it easier for reason and conscience to gain strength and restore balance in the mental processes.

As we recognize the relationship between body and mind, we should also remember the importance of healthy living. A healthy lifestyle directly affects our mental state because the healthier our body, the healthier and more efficient our mind. Conversely, an unhealthy lifestyle prevents us from attaining our full mental potential because it undermines healthy brain function. That is the reason for the health laws given in the Bible. God wants His people to have the healthiest minds possible, but achieving this requires the healthiest bodies possible.

[1] Max B. Kelz et al., "Expression of the Transcription Factor FosB in the Brain Controls Sensitivity to Cocaine," *Nature* 401 (Sept. 16, 1999): 272-276.

[2] B. S. Centerwall, "Television and Violence," *Journal of the American Medical Association* 267 (1992): 3059-3063.

[3] D. Christakis et al., "Early Television Exposure and Subsequent Attentional Problems in Children," *Pediatrics* 113, no. 4 (2004): 708-713.

[4] M. Egan et al., "The Human Genome: Mutations," *American Journal of Psychiatry* 159, no. 1 (2002): 12.

[5] The brain consists of billions of neurons (brain cells) arranged in complex networks. The individual brain cells communicate to each other by releasing chemical signals called neurotransmitters. After the cell sending the signal releases its neurotransmitter, it quickly activates reuptake pumps (like vacuum cleaners) to suck up the neurotransmitter for repackaging and reuse. In areas of the brain where reuptake pumps are sparser, some of the released neurotransmitters remain in the fluid outside the cells. The brain has enzymes designed to remove the leftover neurotransmitters to prevent an overload or buildup.

The prefrontal cortex, the part of the brain immediately behind the forehead, is where we do our thinking and reasoning. The prefrontal cortex has fewer reuptake pumps, so more neurotransmitters remain outside the cells after stimulation. One particular neurotransmitter, dopamine, is important for sharp thinking and good memory. The enzyme that breaks down dopamine is called catechol-O-methyltransferase (COMT). The gene that produces COMT is located on chromosome 22. Dr. Egan and associates have discovered that a random mutation for the gene that makes COMT on chromosome 22 has entered the human gene pool. Therefore, two genetic forms of the gene can be found: one form with the amino acid valine (val) at position 108 on the gene; the other with the amino acid methionine (met) at position 108.

Because each person has two sets of chromosomes (one from his mother and one from his father), three possible genetic combinations exist: met/met, met/val, val/val. Interestingly, the COMT with a met gene is heat-sensitive and shows lower activity at body temperature. Therefore, persons with either the met/met or met/val combination have lower activity of COMT, and subsequently higher levels of dopamine in their prefrontal cortex than those with the val/val combination. Memory testing has revealed that persons with the val/val combination perform worse on short-term memory tests than those with the met gene. And those with the met/met combination perform better than those with the met/val combination. This study has demonstrated that a single gene mutation can directly affect brain chemistry, with subsequent alteration in memory function.

CHAPTER 4

The Balance Upset

The previous two chapters explored a model of the original hierarchical structure of the mind and how the destructive element of selfishness has infected the mind. In this chapter we will examine what happens when the mind operates in reverse order of its original design. We will discover what happens when we allow selfish desires to be in charge. Also we will continue our search for how to restore balance and to heal the mind.

A New Mother

Imagine yourself as a new mother. One week has passed since the birth of your first child. Now you're home alone, and your husband is working out of town for the week. You rise early; attend to the baby; work a long day cleaning the house; and at 11:30 p.m. crawl into bed exhausted.

At 2:00 a.m. your baby, wet and hungry, begins to cry. Do you *feel* like getting out of bed and caring for your infant? No, but you quickly *reason* through your baby's needs and your responsibility to him or her. Your *conscience* convicts you of your duty, and you literally will yourself up to feed and care for the child. Then you go back to bed and sleep the rest of the night.

When you get up the next morning, how do you regard yourself? With a sense of satisfaction, job well done. Maybe a little parental pride. "I'm a really good mom." Your self-esteem rises a little, your self-confidence increases, and your overall sense of well-being remains intact.

But let's reverse the order of supremacy, and instead of letting reason and conscience lead, we'll let *feelings* be in charge. It's 2:00 a.m., and your baby begins to cry. You don't *feel* like getting up, so you don't. Rolling over with a pillow over your head, you remind yourself how much you deserve your rest. In fact, you might even tell yourself you'll be a better parent in the morning because you will be well rested. The next morning you get up to find the child exhausted from crying all night and still wet and hungry. Now how do you experience yourself? Filled with guilt and shame? Perhaps unable to endure such emotions, you look at your child and say, "This is all your fault. If it weren't for you, I wouldn't be in this predicament." What happens to your self-esteem? your self-worth? Do you have a greater sense of peace and well-being?

When feelings are allowed to control the will, it will always lead to destruction.

A Cheerleader

Think about a 16-year-old cheerleader for a high school football team. She has her eye set on the captain of the team. Every time he goes by, she jumps a little higher and cheers a little louder, hoping he will notice. Finally he does, and he asks her out on a date. And on their very first date he attempts to violate her virtue. Her reason and conscience both immediately say, "No, I don't want to do this. I'm not that kind of girl." But her *feelings* are confused and uncertain. *I don't want him to be mad at me,* she tells herself. *I want him to like me. I don't want to be rejected.* And the fear of rejection and the longing to be loved tempt her to give in.

If she goes with her reason and conscience and tells him no, in that moment, alone in the car, how will she feel? Awkward, uncomfortable, anxious, tense? But how will she experience herself during the next week, month, and year? Will her self-esteem go up or down? What if she lets feelings lead and she goes along with his desires, passively allowing him to have his way? Then what would happen to her self-esteem, self-worth, and self-confidence? All down. When feelings take charge, turmoil and destruction always result.

Reflect a moment on your life and consider your 10 most regrettable actions—what you wish you could undo or wish you'd never done. How many of those occurred after a reasonable and conscientious review of the facts and circumstances? How many were based on feelings? Every person—without an exception—to whom I have posed these questions has conceded that most of the time the latter was the case.

A Pastor's Wife

The first two analogies demonstrate the devastating impact on one's self-esteem, self-worth, and self-confidence when feelings are in charge.

But some might counter that the damage resulted because moral violations occurred, not simply because feelings were in charge. These might argue that even if feelings are in charge of decisions, nothing bad will occur if those decisions don't violate morals. If you share that thought, consider the story of Ethel.

The woman came to see me seeking help with chronic feelings of depression, low self-esteem, and insecurity. As the wife of a local pastor, she was ashamed to seek my services. Ethel and her husband had been in the ministry for almost 30 years and had served many churches. As the wife of the pastor, she had on numerous occasions counseled struggling church members, but now she had been unable to find peace for her own heart.

She described how she was raised in a religious household by strict but loving parents. While she could identify no instances of classic abuse in her childhood home, her parents had strictly regulated her behavior and criticized her for any activities that strayed from their zealous ideals. They never encouraged Ethel to ask questions or think for herself. Instead, she was told simply to follow the directions of her parents and God.

Having been raised to be extremely sensitive to criticism, she constantly craved the approval and acceptance of others. But that made it nearly impossible for her to speak her mind or stand up for herself lest she offend someone and then face rejection.

Ethel was kind, patient, generous, and generally loved and respected by everyone. No one in her church could remember a time that she had been rude or unkind. Yet the woman felt lonely, isolated, unappreciated, and depressed. Despite her many years of serving others and doing what she believed was God's will, she couldn't understand why she continued to suffer from chronic insecurity and low self-esteem.

During our sessions together Ethel described one incident that revealed the underlying problem in her life. Taking some classes at a local college, she had final exams scheduled on a Thursday and planned to set aside Wednesday evening of exam week for her final study preparation. On Tuesday of exam week, Doris, the church organist, called to inform her that she would not be able to play the organ for midweek worship and asked if Ethel would play.

In her reason and conscience Ethel immediately concluded that she needed to study Wednesday night and that she didn't want to play the organ for church. Just as quickly, though, a torrent of feelings seemed to overwhelm her: *I don't want Doris to be angry with me. I want her to like me.*

She might think I don't support the church and my husband's ministry. And based on her fear of rejection and what others might think, Ethel decided to cancel her study plans and play the organ instead.

What happened to Ethel's self-esteem? self-confidence? self-worth? They all fell. Not because playing the organ at church is immoral—in fact, it is quite a healthy activity, when done for the right reasons. But her self-esteem plummeted because she made a decision based on feelings of fear and insecurity, not on truth and facts. She went against her own judgment and allowed emotions of fear and insecurity to control her. In her own mind she experienced herself as weak and vacillating. As a consequence, she lost respect for herself.

Fortunately, Ethel soon recognized her longstanding pattern of unhealthy decision-making. For years she had based her responses on what she thought would please others rather than on what she thought would be most reasonable and healthy. She recognized that she had not developed the ability to reason for herself, but instead had allowed others to do the thinking for her. It led to a self-perpetuating cycle of lowered self-esteem, causing a growing need for the approval of others. Also it resulted in an increased fear of rejection, which in turn produced more fear-based decision-making and ever lower self-esteem. When Ethel began to tolerate the disapproval or disappointment of others and made decisions that were reasonable and healthy—simply because *they were* reasonable *and healthy*—her self-esteem and self-worth began to rise.

What enabled her to change? God, as the source of all truth, was shining truth all around her. But truth is useless unless understood and applied. Ethel began exercising her reason and conscience to think for herself and to draw conclusions for herself. She began to search for and apply the truth to her life through exercising her will to act for herself and make her own choices, regardless of what others thought. In other words, she was aware of her feelings of fear, hurt, loneliness, and longing for approval, but recognized that continued surrender to such emotions only perpetuated her problems. That the continual surrender to her feelings was a rejection of truth and only prevented her healing. The diagram on the following page illustrates this battle.

"Am I Supposed to Pretend That I Don't Have Feelings?"

Many of my patients have a very difficult time establishing reason and conscience in governance of the will because their feelings are so strong and they have relied on feelings their entire lives as the basis for their decision-making. They often tell me that until they feel right about something, it isn't real. With a sense of desperation they ask, "Am I supposed to pretend that I don't have feelings?"

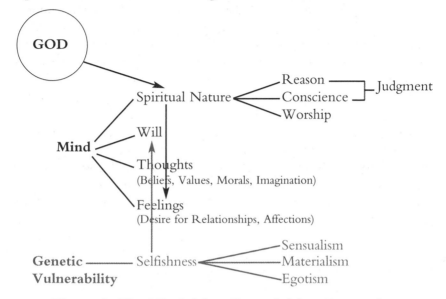

Figure 4. The Mind After Sin and After Conversion

Not at all. Remember the analogy in which you have just come home with your new baby? Place yourself at home with your new infant again at 2:00 a.m. This time, though, instead of the child crying, the phone rings, and it's your closest friend, who is at an all-night movie and wants you to join her. Your feelings quickly shout, "No! Sleep!" Your reason immediately examines your feelings in light of the circumstance. In conjunction with a clear conscience, you decline the offer, gratify your feelings, and return to sleep. Notice, however, that even in this situation feelings are not in control. Reason and conscience make the decision based on facts, evidence, and truth as, given the current circumstances, you decide what is most reasonable and appropriate.

I remind my patients that feelings are data, information that we must let reason and conscience evaluate and then act upon, based not merely on the feelings themselves, but on the facts, evidence, truth, and circumstances associated with the feeling.

Feelings Can Lie!

What essentially all of my patients do not realize when they first come

41

to see me is that *feelings can lie!* So many people mistakenly believe that if it *feels* right, it must *be* right. But the Bible says in James 1:13, 14: "When tempted, no one should say, 'God is tempting me.' For God cannot be tempted by evil, nor does he tempt anyone; but each one is tempted when, by his own evil desire" [or feelings], he is dragged away and enticed." The passage informs us that it is through our feelings that we most commonly get led astray.

Alice was desperate when she arrived for her first appointment. Her hair was blond, frizzy, and sticking up in all directions, and her makeup was too heavy. Moderately overweight, she wore jeans two sizes too small, accented by a pullover t-shirt with a glitter-emblazoned picture of a monster truck. She wore bright-red nail polish and lipstick that extended beyond the margins of her lips. Each hand had at least seven rings, two eyebrow rings bobbed above her right eye, and multiple ear studs rimmed each ear. She smelled of tobacco and looked 50, but was actually just 37.

In our initial sessions her comments were difficult to follow as she jumped from topic to topic and problem to problem. Whenever we attempted to deal with one problem, she would immediately present several more in a frantic recitation of helpless hopelessness. Her life was chaotic, with no focus and no evidence of self-control. She did whatever her feelings motivated her to do. Married to her third husband and with three children, she considered her life miserable, but she had no idea of how she might improve it. Suffering from extremely low self-esteem and chronic feelings of worthlessness, she could not recall a time that she had been happy or at peace with herself.

After I shared with Alice the hierarchy of the mind and the importance of fact-based rather than feeling-based decision-making, she began to comprehend the principles and made some modest gains. Unfortunately, just as she was beginning to show real improvement, everything threatened to fall apart.

One day she disclosed her attraction to her best friend's husband. She stated that she longed to have an affair with him, something that she repeated numerous times throughout the session: "But Dr. Jennings, it would feel so good." So I began to ask her some reality-based questions.

"Would it *be* good for your husband if you have an affair with your best friend's husband?"

"No."

"Would it *be* good for your best friend if you have an affair with her

42

husband?" Again she answered no. "Would it *be* good for your kids? her kids? And ultimately would it *be* good for you and her husband?" Each time she reluctantly answered no.

By now she realized that she had to choose between two options: She could accept the facts that reason and conscience had determined would be most healthy, resulting in her not pursuing such an affair. Or she could follow her feelings, choosing to engage in an ill-advised relationship.

What do you think would happen to her self-esteem, self-confidence, and self-worth if she had the affair? What do you think would happen to her mood? Alice struggled with her decision, but eventually chose to follow reason and conscience. She decided to exercise her will and not pursue the affair. Guess what? Within two weeks her feelings toward the man had completely vanished, and her level of self-confidence continued to climb.

CHAPTER 5

The Law of Liberty

"No man has received from nature the right to give orders to others.
Freedom is a gift from heaven, and every individual of the same species
has the right to enjoy it as soon as he is in enjoyment
of his reason."—Denis Diderot.

Joni seemed to be a frightened child—hurting, longing for comfort, for help, yet afraid to reach out, terrified lest she be hurt again. Her hands trembled nervously, and her dark eyes darted back and forth, clearly seeking to avoid meeting my gaze. The striking features of the 23-year-old woman showed traces of childlike innocence hidden behind a wall of pain and fear. She spoke softly and hesitantly, her voice quivering uneasily. As I escorted her down the hall to my office, I thought, *What will she tell me? What could be troubling her so? Why does she seem so frightened, so insecure?*

Entering my office, she immediately broke down and began to sob. Tearfully she described how she had once been an outgoing vibrant young woman who thought nothing of organizing her friends for a weekend outing or giving a presentation at school. With a slight smile she told me of being president of her senior class. She remembered when she had been popular, energetic, and fun-loving, but all of that had changed when, at age 19, she had married her high school sweetheart. During the first few months their relationship had seemed perfect, but soon after the honeymoon her husband had begun drinking, and over the years he had become increasingly demanding, critical, and controlling.

If Joni wanted to go out with one of her friends, he forbade her, and if she attempted to resist his demands, he became hostile and threatening. Whenever he took the notion, he ordered her—regardless of what she was doing—to strip and lie down where she was so that he could gratify himself. If she said no, he hit her. Finally she stopped resisting and instead submitted whenever he commanded.

By the time Joni came to see me she was depressed, confused, insecure, uncertain, fearful, unhappy, and hopeless. The startling change in her marriage had completely demoralized her. She neither understood what had gone wrong nor knew what to do about it. In this universe we have a law—ordained by God Himself—called the law of liberty. It is not a rule or a legislative enactment or an arbitrary command by a powerful potentate. Rather, it is a universal reality, as with the law of gravity. Think about the law of gravity. You don't have to know about it for it to work. Nor do you have to believe in the law of gravity to feel its effects. In fact, you can deny that it exists at all. But if you ride the elevator to the top of the Empire State Building, proclaim that no such thing as the law of gravity exists, and then jump off, you will quickly find yourself under the jurisdiction of the law whose reality you deny. Violating the law of gravity has accompanying consequences, whether or not one anticipates them.

The law of liberty works in a similar manner, regardless of whether one believes in, acknowledges, or recognizes it. And violations of the law of liberty always result in damaging consequences in very predictable ways.

A Proposal Without Freedom

Imagine the case of a young woman dating the man of her dreams. One day after they have known each other for several months he takes her to a special restaurant and then out for a romantic walk in the garden. With soft music in the background he kneels down and asks her to marry him.

Realizing the importance of the decision, the young woman asks for a few moments to contemplate her answer. Her hesitancy making him insecure, he reaches into his pocket and pulls out a pistol, points it at her head, and states, "Look, I've taken you out, bought you flowers and gifts, and spent my time and money on you. Now, you better marry me and you better love me, because if you don't, I will shoot you where you stand."

What do you think happens in the young woman's heart? "Oh! You're the strong man I've been waiting for"? Of course not. We all recognize that such treatment would cause fear, revulsion, and disgust, ultimately resulting in rebellion. She would want to get away from him as soon as possible.

Our illustration reveals the first two predictable consequences that occur when someone violates the law of liberty: *it always destroys love and incites rebellion.* It happens wherever and in whatever circumstances our freedoms get violated.

Lasagna

Consider a wife who wants to surprise her husband with his favorite dish. After working for several hours to prepare her special lasagna that she knows he loves, she puts it in the oven so that it will be ready when he arrives home from work.

But on the way home he calls his wife and announces, "I've had a horrible day at work. I want some lasagna, so get yourself into the kitchen and make it. And it better be ready when I get home." Not waiting for a response, he hangs up.

What type of reaction would you expect from the wife? She knows that the lasagna is already cooking in the oven. Do you think she would now want to throw it out? Would her husband's violation of her freedom cause a rebellious reaction? Love perishes and rebellion springs up whenever freedom is violated.

"I'll Have a Coke."

Now imagine being out at a restaurant with your spouse. The server asks what you would like to drink. You reply, "I'll have a Coke." But immediately your spouse states, "She can't have Coke—bring her milk." How would you respond? Would this violation of liberty increase love or decrease it? Would you find yourself drawn closer to your spouse or pushed away?

All violations of the law of liberty have the same result: the destruction of love and fomenting of rebellion.. The only variable is in degree. Greater violations of liberty have more devastating results. In the case of gravity, tumble off a four-inch curb, and you might merely twist an ankle. But fall off a 40-foot building, and you will likely die. The law of gravity applies to each instance, the only variable being the degree of damage that occurs.

Why Did God Use so Much Force?

God has gone to great lengths to demonstrate to us that the violation of liberty does not restore love. Once He employed His power to destroy the entire world with a flood (Gen. 6-11). It was an incredible use of power, but did it lead to loyalty and restored unity with humanity? After the Flood, why did people build the Tower of Babel? Because they didn't believe there was a God, or because they didn't trust Him never to destroy the world again?

God used His power to kill the firstborn of Egypt (Ex. 11:1-12:30) and then overwhelm Pharaoh's army in the sea (Ex. 14:23-28). The Lord thundered from Sinai with grand displays of might, and all the children of Israel were afraid (Ex. 20:18, 19). When God demonstrated His power in such ways, did restored unity result? Or did rebellion and worshipping a golden calf follow (Ex. 32:1-8)?

At Mount Carmel, Elijah called fire down from heaven, and all the people fell on their faces and exclaimed, "The Lord—he is God! The Lord—he is God!" (1 Kings 18:39). But after that awesome display of power, did the people of Israel react with perpetual loyalty and faithfulness? Or did they respond with recurrent rebellion and idolatry (see the books of Isaiah, Jeremiah, Amos, Hosea, and Micah)?

God says through the prophet Zechariah, "Not by might nor by power, but by my Spirit, says the Lord" (Zech. 4:6). And how does the Spirit work? Through love, truth, and freedom. It is by revealing truth in love and by leaving us free to come to our own conclusion that God wins the heart (Eph. 4:15).

Love Requires Freedom

When Lucifer rebelled (see Isa. 14; Eze. 28), God did not employ His might to force the angel to conform. God did not use His power to punish and destroy. Instead, He avoided force, because it is contrary to His methods and principles. In His omniscience God realizes that using coercion only incites greater rebellion. It does not restore unity and harmony or love. Love requires freedom.

Emergency Measures

If might and power don't accomplish God's goal of unity, then why did He employ so much of it in the Old Testament? God took great risks of being misunderstood by His use of it in the past. During emergency situations, great love will take great risks. But we shouldn't mistake emergency measures as a violation of the law of liberty.

Located in the northwest corner of Georgia, Cloudland Canyon State Park takes its name from the beautiful view seen from the tops of the steep canyon walls. Imagine that your family takes a trip to such a place. Your children are laughing and playing when you notice your son chasing a Frisbee that is sailing for the cliff. What would you do? Would you shout? Certainly. So you shout, "Stop—the cliff!" But he is so caught up in what he is doing that he doesn't hear you. So you yell louder, but the wind is blowing and whips away your words. As he approaches the cliff, do you scream at the top of your lungs in an effort to save his life? Of course you do: "STOP NOW! I SAID STOP!" Finally your concern prevails, but it is also misunderstood. Four hikers across the canyon hear you and think, *What a cruel parent. I would never treat my child like that.*

Do we sometimes take risks of being misunderstood in emergency circumstances? Consider the immense risks God took when He raised His voice in the past.

Put yourself in the place of a teacher in an elementary school who has just brought the kids back from recess. They are still laughing and making noise when you get the word that a gunman is lurking in the building and you need to evacuate immediately. When you call for attention, the children don't hear because they are too loud. Do you raise your voice and yell if necessary to quiet them, restore order, and direct them to safety? Do you risk this behavior—clearly uncharacteristic of you—even if some of the students go home and tell their parents that the teacher yelled at them?

As a U.S. troopship crossed the Atlantic during World War II, a torpedo struck it, and it began slowly sinking. The soldiers were billeted below deck, and many of those compartments began to flood. The deck hatch was opened, and the panic-stricken men below frantically tried to escape. As one soldier attempted to climb the ladder to reach the deck, two or three others ripped him off and another jumped on the ladder, only to be pulled off by several more below. All were fighting in terror for the one ladder leading to the deck.

On deck were the officers, who shouted for order, but the men below, in their panic, didn't hear. Because the water was continuing to rise, all the men were in danger of perishing if order didn't get restored soon. Suddenly a burst of gunfire rang through the air as one of the officers on deck took a rifle and shot down into the compartment, killing several soldiers. But his action immediately stopped the panic, and the rest were saved.

The Beginning of Wisdom

God took great risks in using His might and power—not because He preferred to do things that way, but because of the emergencies He was dealing with. Proverbs states, "The fear of the Lord is the beginning of wisdom" (9:10)—not the end of wisdom. When you are out of control—worshipping a golden calf and participating in an orgy at the foot of Sinai—divine thundering might cause you to stop your destructive behavior long enough to listen. The message to each of us is this: If you listen to God and spend time with Him, you will discover, as did Moses, that there is no need to be afraid (see Ex. 20:20).

When anything violates our freedom, it always leads to rebellion and the unavoidable destruction of love. It is impossible for love to exist in an atmosphere without freedom. If you're not sure, try it on your spouse. Tell him or her that if they don't love you, you will kill them. Restrict your spouse's liberties, and see what then happens to love.

The law of liberty is one of the cornerstone principles of God's government. As God is love, He necessarily *must* respect the liberty and individuality of His intelligent creatures. To do otherwise would destroy love and incite rebellion.

Saul of Tarsus Didn't Understand

The law of liberty was a truth that even the apostle Paul didn't initially understand. Prior to his conversion on the Damascus road Paul was known as Saul of Tarsus—and what were his methods for reclaiming the followers of Christ? Saul evangelized with an escort of the Temple guard who used force, coercion, torture, and imprisonment in an attempt to turn Christians back to traditional Judaism. He even held the coats of those who stoned the first martyr, Stephen (Acts 7:57-8:1).

But after his experience on the Damascus road, when disputes over religious matters arose, Paul wrote in Romans 14:5: "Let all be fully convinced in their own minds" (NRSV). In other words, present the truth in love and then leave people free to make up their own minds (Eph. 4:15). Before he became an apostle of Christ Paul used the methods of Satan, but after his encounter with the Savior his methods changed and he practiced the law of liberty.

Christ and the Law of Liberty

If violations of the law of liberty *always* result in the destruction of love and in rebellion, then why didn't Jesus stop loving when someone violated His freedoms? When Christ was bound, beaten, and crucified, why did He not stop loving—if, indeed, the violation of freedom *always* destroys love?

We find the answer in His voluntary surrender to abuse: Christ never lost His freedom. Christ was not crucified against His will, but in accordance with His will.

In Gethsemane Christ had surrendered His fate into His Father's hands and prayed, "Not as I will, but as you will" (Matt. 26:39, NIV). When Peter suggested that Christ not submit to the cross, Christ rebuked him (Matt. 16:23). Christ was determined to go to the cross.

And when Peter struck the high priest's servant, cutting off his ear,

Christ again chastised Peter, restored the man's ear, and stated that if He did ask His Father, 12 legions of angels would be sent from heaven to rescue Him (Matt. 26:52, 53). In fact, Jesus explicitly stated that no one could take His life, but that He would lay it down voluntarily (John 10:17).

Because He voluntarily laid down His life, Christ's freedom was never violated. No creature could take away the liberty of God. The only way Christ could have been crucified was if He voluntarily submitted. Therefore, rather than destroying love, the cross was God's method of bringing His love to us.

The first two predictable consequences of violating the law of liberty are the destruction of love and the incitement of rebellion. But if rebellion fails to restore freedom, then the third predictable consequence of violating the law of liberty occurs. We will explore it in the next chapter.

CHAPTER 6

Shadow People

*"The shallow consider liberty a release from all law, from every constraint.
The wise man sees in it, on the contrary, the potent
Law of Laws."—Walt Whitman.*

Shirley's family physician had sent her to see me because he was worried she might be suffering from depression. Getting a history from the 46-year-old woman was quite difficult. She sat with her hands between her legs, avoided all eye contact, and spoke in quiet tones with essentially no modulation to her voice.

If she responded at all, she tended to answer most questions with "I don't know" or "I guess." After long minutes of silence and patient questioning, this modestly obese woman who dressed rather plainly began to disclose her painful history of physical abuse by her husband.

Hesitantly she described one incident in which her husband told her he wanted dinner ready at 5:00 p.m.: she had worked diligently preparing the meal, but served it at 5:02 p.m. She cried as she related that her husband had begun to beat her, breaking her nose and blackening her eye. And while he was punching her, he stated, "I hate it when you make me do this. Why do you make me do this? If you would only serve dinner when you're supposed to, I wouldn't have to hit you. Don't you know I only do this for your own good, because I love you?"

As Shirley recounted her ordeal, I made a comment criticizing her husband for his behavior. It was then that she looked up and made eye contact with me for the first time and said, "Oh no! It wasn't his fault. If I would have had dinner ready on time, he wouldn't have had to hit me."

The third predictable consequence when one surrenders to the violation of the law of liberty is that it will destroy individuality. When a person submits to the control of another for a sufficient period of time, it slowly erodes both his or her unique identity and the ability to think and reason for oneself. The submissive individual begins to think through the eyes of the controlling person rather than with his or her own mind.

Shirley was not an unusual case. No longer thinking for herself, she had surrendered her identity to her abusive husband and accepted his version of reality as her own. She had become little more than a shadow of her husband. Not only does the violation of freedom destroy love; if rebellion doesn't restore freedom, then individuality itself vanishes and only shadows remain.

Most Violations of Liberty Are Not Obvious

Most of the violations of liberty are not as obvious as what Shirley experienced, yet they are just as destructive.

John was a small man in his late 50s. His hair was white, long on the left, and combed over the top in a useless attempt to cover his receding hairline. Although he had attended college briefly after high school, he was a self-taught individual, a person of significant intelligence and experience.

A senior foreman for a large construction company, he had been involved in the trade from an early age. He ran several large crews and had recently received a handsome bonus for his outstanding work. But John was troubled; his eyes were sad with a sense of regret, and worry furrowed his brow. His voice had a deep rumble like a train in the distance, but it echoed with a hollow sound of loneliness.

The father of three successful sons, he had been married to his only wife for more than 30 years. His business continued to be successful and his health was good, yet he came to see me depressed, hopeless, insecure, and suffering from discouragement and lack of self-esteem. Terribly confused, he thought he should be happy—after all, he had no significant problems—yet his depression continued to worsen.

As we talked John reported that during an argument early in their marriage, his wife had threatened to leave him. Because the threat had seriously frightened him, he backed down and placated his wife. He described scenario after scenario in which he had evaluated a situation and reached his own conclusion, but since it differed from his wife's opinion, he had gone along with her out of fear of her response. Would she become upset, sullen, make a scene, not speak for days, or, worst of all, leave him?

Through 30 years of marriage he had lived in constant fear. Despite his success at work, he came home and considered himself a failure. Regardless of how clearly he thought and how effectively he made decisions outside of the home, he was seldom "right" when he arrived home.

John reported that although he frequently disagreed with his wife, he never expressed it. He described many occasions he had declined offers from his coworkers who had asked him to play a round of golf or watch a ball game. Instead of thinking, *Do I have any conflicts in my schedule?* John thought, *What will my wife think? Will she be mad? I wonder if she will let me go.* No longer thinking for himself, he filtered his thoughts through his wife's mind. Slowly John was losing his individuality, his ability to think for himself. In the process he had become a shadow of his wife.

Unfortunately, the law of liberty is poorly understood and frequently broken. And all too often it is violated in the name of Christ. How sad He must be to have persons take His name while they use force, intimidation, and control to achieve their goals.

Violations of Liberty in Christ's Name

During my residency I counseled a 35-year-old Hispanic woman, belonging to a Pentecostal denomination, who had suffered with depression for many years. As we worked together, Sophie disclosed how her particular culture and faith group expected women to subordinate themselves to their husbands. Her denomination would not permit women to speak in her church. If she had a question, she must wait until she was back home to ask her husband. Nor did any of the church's committees or boards include women.

At home she experienced similar treatment. The husband was head of the home, and the wife was to do his bidding. Repeatedly she heard that God had designed society in this way for two reasons: woman had been deceived and had led man into sin, and though God had created man in the image of God, He had made women in the image of man. Through the years she had surrendered to the constant degradation of women and had permitted her husband to control her.

As is the case anytime the law of liberty is violated, Sophie had significant amounts of unresolved anger and resentment toward her husband as well as the deity who would ordain such a system. Also she found it extremely difficult to think for herself and had lost much of her confidence, esteem, and worth. As her individuality slowly faded away, she was silently dying inside. She was in the process of becoming a shadow person, a pale imitation of her husband.

As we worked together, Sophie came to understand the principles of the law of liberty and began to apply them to her life. Shortly after she began to reason for herself and to exercise her individuality and autonomy, though, her husband intruded into one of our sessions.

Marching in with his Bible in hand, he slammed it down on my desk and said, "Tell my wife the Bible says a wife is to be submissive to her husband!" As he said it I noticed Sophie's body posture change. Prior to her husband's entrance she had seemed at ease—sitting up, bright-eyed, smiling, and talking without hesitation. But as her husband made his demands, she slowly sank down in her chair, her head slumped so that her chin touched her chest, her shoulders rolled inward, and she brought her hands in between her legs. She had assumed the appearance of a sad, scared child, and it was absolutely clear to me that she feared that her hope of freedom was about to be destroyed.

To her husband I responded, "It's true that the Bible teaches that wives are to submit to their husbands. But if you read the very next verse, the Bible also states that husbands are to treat their wives as Christ treated the church, sacrificing himself for her [see Eph. 5:22-25]. Now when you begin sacrificing yourself for your wife's happiness, I'm sure she will have no problem submitting to that type of treatment."

As I spoke I noticed that she sat up straight, thrust her shoulders back, and wore a big smile. Fortunately for Sophie, her husband really desired to do what was right, but was himself a victim of serious misconceptions about God and His methods. He accepted the redirection given and began attending marital therapy. Together they developed a healthy, mutually rewarding relationship that respected individuality and autonomy.

Marriage and the Law of Liberty

Unfortunately, many good people suffer ignorantly within marriages that cruelly violate the laws of love and liberty, believing they are required to stay in such destructive situations. But God has never required this. His purpose for us has only and always been our healing and restoration. Therefore, He desires our separation from everything that interferes with His working in our lives.

What is the greatest of all the commandments? Jesus replied: "'Love the Lord your God with all your heart and with all your soul and with all your mind.' This is the first and greatest commandment. And the second is like it: 'Love your neighbor as yourself.' All the Law and the Prophets hang on these two commandments" (Matt. 22:37-40).

Where does a spouse fall? In the "God" or in the "neighbor" category? Clearly a spouse is not God. Our responsibility is always to Him first, and to spouse second. How much better would our world be if Adam had remembered this fact before he accepted the forbidden fruit. Our responsibility is to present ourselves to God in the best condition, for the greatest usefulness possible.

Marriage relationships that cause or allow freedom, individuality, and autonomy to erode will result in the destruction of the image of God within. And if freedom is not restored, one's fitness for heaven will be ruined. It is one of Satan's most subtle traps.

When love and freedom cannot be restored within the marriage; when staying in the marriage results in individuals being so dominated and controlled that it erases their individuality and autonomy, then they have a God-given responsibility to extricate themselves from such destructive relationships.

Many wives wrongly believe that they are to submit blindly to the leadership of their husbands (and many husbands promote this false belief to maintain unhealthy control over their wives). But as we have previously discussed, God does not expect wives to submit blindly to their husbands. Instead, Scripture calls them to submit to Christlike treatment from their husbands.

How has Christ treated the church? He gave constantly of Himself for the good of His people. Always seeking the good of others, He led by example, not by power and authority. Christ has invited us to become His thinking, understanding friends, not mindless slaves simply doing as instructed (John 15:15). Our Savior works by revealing truth in love and leaving us free to choose whether or not to follow His leading.

God does not want us to surrender our minds to Him for His direct control. He does not want to be a puppet master with us as the puppets. Such a relationship would destroy love. But He does want us to surrender our hearts and minds to Him for cleansing and restoration, and then only when we are convinced, by the weight of evidence, that He is indeed trustworthy. Healing us, He sets us free to be self-governed, self-controlled individuals operating in harmony with His methods of love and liberty (Gal. 5:22, 23).

Likewise, wives are not to submit their identity to their husbands for the husband to control. In fact, husbands are to build up the individuality of the wife and promote the recovery of the image of God within her. A husband should not restrict her liberties, but should help his wife improve her ability to think and reason for herself. We are to be thinkers, not reflectors of another's thoughts, not shadows of another. Husbands are to invite their wives into understanding friendship to be intelligent partners, to be coequals in worth, love, loyalty, devotion, and authority, all the while cooperating together for their mutual good.

God Hates the Loss of His Children

God created humans in His image so that they could reveal truth about Himself. He designed marriage to demonstrate Godlike love. Divorce is the outworking of selfishness, and it occurs when love breaks down. Because divorce results in pain and injury to His children, God hates divorce (Mal. 2:16). However, *what God detests even more than divorce is the destruction and eternal loss of His children.* Marriages that perpetually violate love and liberty are gross counterfeits of the benevolent principles of God's character. Such marriages masquerade as bastions of love, while misrepresenting Him and destroying both husband and wife.

Hypnosis Violates the Law of Liberty

The violation of the law of liberty can occur in many settings. The most destructive, however, are those that present themselves as bulwarks of safety, such as families, churches, or health-care practices. As we discovered earlier, whenever anything shatters the law of liberty, predictable patterns of destruction will occur, regardless of setting or intention.

Many of my patients have asked to be hypnotized or have asked if hypnosis works. In fact, it can have profound impact on the mind. The more important question relates to whether hypnosis actually brings healing or instead enfeebles the mental faculties.

Hypnosis is the process of suspending one's reasoning abilities and allowing a third party to make suggestions, give direction, implant beliefs, or affect memories that the mind will then accept without critical examination. It is the process of bypassing the highest faculties of reason and conscience and directly accessing the beliefs, memories, morals, values, and imagination. Further, it detaches the spiritual nature from its role in overseeing the formation of our beliefs, values, morals, and use of imagination. Hypnosis trains the mind to accept suggestions without critically examining them for reliability.

The things we believe have powerful effects on our well-being. Therefore, to the degree that hypnosis can change our beliefs, it can significantly alter a person's experience. One of the most fundamental problems related to hypnosis is that it alters beliefs without utilizing one's God-given reasoning powers to examine one's beliefs, weigh the evidences, and freely choose the course that strengthens reason and ennobles the individual. Instead, hypnosis puts others in charge of the mind and surrenders individuality to them. This weakens the reasoning powers, making it more difficult to establish and maintain the mental hierarchy God has designed.

Scripture teaches (Heb. 5:11–6:4; Eph. 4:14, 15) that mature Christians are those who have developed the ability to discern right from wrong, the healthy from the unhealthy, the good from the bad. Hypnosis impairs this ability because it trains a person to sideline reason and conscience, while trusting another to direct the mental faculties.

God Would Never Use Hypnosis

Many sincere Christians pray, "Lord, I surrender my *will* to You. You take control. I don't want to be in control anymore." Will God do this? Will God take control of someone's will? Even if asked? Consider this scenario: You obtain nanochip technology that you can inject into your children. Such nanochips would lodge in the brain and establish a network that you can access via your computer using radio transmission. Next, you use your computer to program your children to come to you three times a day and tell you that they love you. Would this be love? As we established earlier, whenever freedom gets violated, love is destroyed.

In no way could programming someone produce genuine love, but it might yield a mere mechanical performance. God will never do this, though, because He is truly love and wants only service and devotion freely given. Hypnosis robs a person of the freedom to think and make informed choices. Rebellion doesn't occur with hypnotic violations of the law of liberty, because the individual undergoing hypnosis has voluntarily surrendered to it. Hypnosis paralyzes, immobilizes, or otherwise inactivates reason and conscience so that the violations of liberty go unrecognized. But hypnosis invariably erodes the individuality and the ability to think and reason independently. It promotes the development of shadow people—people who have lost the ability to think for themselves.

There is a technique that people often confuse with hypnosis but that, unlike hypnosis, can be helpful. The technique is guided imagery. During guided imagery, rather than another directing the faculties of one's mind, the individual retains control over them. Reason and conscience stay in charge, directing the will to activate the imagination. A person can use guided imagery to meditate on God's creation, character, and presence.

God Doesn't Destroy Individuality

Unfortunately the various destructive methods we have looked at can at times be so subtle that we might mistakenly consider them to be the working of God Himself. But He never operates in ways that destroy individuality. In Galatians 5 we find what people become when they work with God for their healing and restoration. They develop characters with specific defining features, which the Bible calls "fruits." And because they arise by the working of the Holy Spirit, Scripture calls them "fruit of the Spirit"—"love, joy, peace, patience, kindness, goodness, faithfulness, gentleness and self-control" (verses 22, 23).

When the Holy Spirit has His way in our lives, we develop self-control and self-governance, rather than operating as divinely controlled puppets. Set free, we do everything according to the principles of God: love, liberty, truth, and openness. It is only in relationship with Christ that one finds true freedom—freedom from fear, freedom from the control of others, freedom from the domination of our genetic weakness.

CHAPTER 7

The Law of Love

"The law of the Lord is perfect,
reviving the soul.
The statutes of the Lord are trustworthy,
making wise the simple."—Ps. 19:7.

When I first began to explore the issue of love, I found myself overwhelmed with possibilities. I knew, as a Christian, that love was central to God's plan to heal humanity, but most of what I read talked about love as some amorphous force or some emotional warm fuzzy. It just didn't seem to make sense. The initial problem I had with exploring the parameters of love was trying to distinguish between love and its counterfeits and then trying not only to experience love but also to understand it. The thought that love was actually a universal law—a principle on which life is based—was so far from my mind that I couldn't even, initially, comprehend the possibility. But as I began to understand the other universal constants, such as the law of liberty, the law of love came more and more into focus.

In the previous two chapters we explored how violations of the law of liberty damage and destroy. We examined the life of Shirley and the consequences she endured as her husband violated her freedoms. Intuitively we recognize that all violations of the law of liberty are violations of love, but we must also grasp the fact that not all violations of the law of love are violations of liberty.

Sam and Wilma had been married for 43 years. They had three adult children and were now supposed to be enjoying retirement. Unfortunately, their marriage was on the verge of collapse, not because of infidelity, physical abuse, or persistent violations of liberty, but because of failing to love—failing to actively think about the good of the other before acting, failing to put the other first.

Both Sam and Wilma were active church members and would never think of doing something that others would consider as flagrant "sin," but they all too often failed to do things that would be regarded as overt "love." Both were constantly seeking to get their needs satisfied rather than seeking to meet those of the other. They had fallen into the trap of indifference, a relationship in which they no longer cared about the other. Instead of simply seeking to love each other, they sought only to get something from the other. They were miserable, their hearts were slowly hardening, and they were emotionally and spiritually dying.

Love is not simply about avoiding injurious activities—it is about choosing to purposefully act in uplifting and selfless ways. Nor is it simply about doing what feels good. Rather, love involves doing what *is* good regardless of how one feels. Doing what is in the best interest of another and giving of oneself for another, love is selfless. When we love, we live. When we stop loving, we die.

Jenny was nervous. She and her husband, Phil, were on their way to take her parents out for lunch. Her 83-year-old father had been suffering from Alzheimer's dementia for several years. As her father's mental abilities declined, his behavior had become more bizarre and could even become irritating to others. How would Phil deal with her father if Dad didn't behave?

As soon as they picked up Jenny's parents, her father began asking Phil what kind of car he had, what year it was built, what kind of gasoline mileage it was getting. He repeated the questions more than 10 times in less than 15 minutes. But rather than get irritated, Phil answered each question with a cheerful, calm, and patient demeanor, showing real concern and compassion for Jenny's father. Phil gave of himself and did what was right because it was right, not because of how it felt. The husband revealed love in action.

Love Is Life

The law of love is the law of life—the principle upon which all life in the universe is based. As God Himself is love, He designed everything that He created to operate in harmony with this law of love, this circle of beneficence in which all things give freely to others. In nature we witness this cycle in the sun warming the oceans, which creates the clouds, which rain on the land to form the lakes, rivers, and streams, which flow through the land bringing life, and ultimately return to the sea to begin the circle again.

The plants produce the oxygen necessary for animals to live, and animals in turn produce carbon dioxide, which plants need to grow. The law of love is the law of life. Even in nature, when giving ceases so does life. The pool of water that stops flowing and releasing its water soon stagnates, and everything in it dies. When we cease to give our breath to benefit the plants, we inevitably die. It is through giving that we live. Those who accept and apply the law of love are themselves preserved from evil. But when we seek only to take, we slowly die. When we stop giving, we cut ourselves off from the channels of blessing—and the unavoidable result is death.

Flowers give their pollen to bees, and bees fertilize the flowers, thus increasing their fruit. Trees bestow their nuts on the squirrels, and squirrels eat, spread, and bury the nuts, thus increasing the number of trees. The law of love is the law of giving—the law of life.

The world, as it came from the hand of God, was perfect, and all nature fully revealed the law of love. But once sin entered the world an antagonistic principle infected nature and obscured the clear revelation of God's love. Once sin, which is the principle of selfishness, marred God's love in nature, it became necessary for Him to provide His Written Word in order for us to see and understand the divine principle clearly.

Those who study nature unaided by the Written Word of God will often fail to see His hand and instead see the infection that has marred His beautiful creation. Naturalists often describe the infection by the famous phrase "survival of the fittest"—the principle of selfishness. Charles Darwin did not invent the principle of survival of the fittest—he merely observed in nature this selfish motive that has scarred God's handiwork, and failed to understand the true meaning of what he saw.

Likewise, psychiatrists and psychologists who study human behavior invariably find themselves focusing on the infection that is destroying humanity and conclude that it is "natural." Freud, having given up his belief in God, made this tragic mistake when he concluded that the central force in human beings is the id, which is simply the infection of selfishness. Without God's Written Word to enlighten the mind and put in proper context what we observe in human nature, many people believe the infection that is destroying the human race is simply a normal, and therefore acceptable, part of our being.

Imagine living in a village in Africa in which the entire population is infected with the AIDS virus and everyone is so uneducated that they have never even heard of the disease. Every child is born infected with it, and every adult suffers from its devastation. Everyone is sick and dying. Imagine that the village gets cut off from the rest of the world, and as the years go by, new generations forget what human life is like without the

AIDS virus. Among them arise naturalists who observe human life. Might they incorrectly conclude that the infection is a natural part of their human condition? Might they and the population as a whole come to believe that it is the way it is supposed to be?

All nature is infected. As Paul said in Romans 8:22, all nature groans under the weight of sin, and viruses offer a perfect example of the effects of such sin. They were not part of God's original creation. How do we know? Because of the law of love. Viruses are based solely on a biological form of selfishness. A virus is a small piece of genetic code (DNA or RNA). It has no ability to give anything, but can only take for itself. When a virus enters a living host, it assumes control of the machinery of the cells and causes them to produce more and more of the virus—self-replication, self-exaltation. And it does this so extensively that, if not checked, it kills the host and then itself because it eventually has no more host to exploit. What an accurate example of the unimpeded course of sin in our lives.

Our white blood cells, on the other hand, are part of God's creation and operate on the principle of love—self-sacrifice. When an infecting agent enters our body, our white blood cells willingly sacrifice themselves in order to save us. What a contrast, even on the cellular level, of the difference between love and selfishness.

Human beings are infected with selfishness, and it is God's plan to remove selfishness as the central motivating principle in the human mind and restore His law of love and liberty as its central operating principle. Unless this healing of mind occurs, the inevitable result is death.

While selfishness currently infects all humanity, God did not leave us to struggle helplessly with our sickness. No! He sent us His Written Word and His Son to reveal His plan to heal us and restore us to our original condition. By reading the text sent by our Creator, we can enhance our ability to distinguish between the infection and what God originally intended our condition to be. We can then make intelligent decisions to cooperate with Him for healing and transformation.

To Violate Love Is Death

Have you ever wondered why God warned Adam that if he ate of the tree he would die? It was because of the law of love, the principle of giving upon which life is based. When one is out of harmony with this law, the unavoidable consequence is death—not because of an angry and vengeful deity, but because violating the law of love cuts a person off from the channel of blessings and as a result life simply cannot continue. Just as a pool of water isolated from its source will stagnate and become lifeless, so the human mind severed from God will perish.

Adam received everything on our planet except one tree and its fruit. God reserved the fruit of that tree and instructed Adam and Eve not to partake of it, but He gave them everything else on earth as their possession. If the first couple valued God's love and wanted to demonstrate their love, would they steal from Him? Would they take what didn't belong to them? Or, if they loved God, would they respect His possession and refrain from eating the fruit that wasn't theirs?

Love means doing what's in the best interest of the other person regardless of how one feels. It is the principle of giving; and stealing from someone violates that principle. Stealing is the opposite of love, the opposite of giving. It is taking, grasping, hoarding. And as soon as Adam broke the law of love by taking for himself and grasping for self-exaltation, he experienced a change. Instead of experiencing a higher nobler state of existence, he became afraid, and his own ability to love was damaged.

When Adam ate the fruit, he severed his unity with God. In the process he chose the principle of self-exaltation, self-seeking, and selfishness, and it replaced the law of love in his mind, closing it to the abundant and continual flow of love from the heart of God. God still loved Adam, but that love no longer lived in Adam's heart.

Once Adam broke the law of love, his entire character changed. Self-seeking replaced the principle of self-sacrificing love, giving, and beneficence, and immediately he was more concerned with himself, his situation, his problems, and his circumstances than anything else. Fear overcame him. His reason was imbalanced, his conscience bruised, and his will now came under the control of his feelings. The principle of "survival of the fittest" now dominated Adam's mind, and he immediately ran and hid and tried to blame Eve for his condition (see Gen. 3:12). Adam had lost the ability to love. Without divine intervention, his condition was terminal.

Falling Dominoes of Destruction

Any violation of the law of love produces an immediate cascade of predictable consequences. Like knocking over a series of dominoes, once the first domino falls the rest immediately follow. Inevitable damage occurs. And the first consequence is that it damages our own ability to love. We no longer naturally seek to give to others, but instead find ourselves driven to get for ourselves.

Breaking the law of love not only damages our faculties of reason and conscience, but also begins convicting us of wrongdoing. We experience such self-incrimination as fear, anxiety, and insecurity, causing us to lose the ability to think clearly. But instead of recognizing that the problem is in us, we misjudge God and try to hide ourselves from Him. Instead of realizing that we are sick and dying, many actually believe that God wants to punish us. Such misjudgment of God causes us to close our minds to the channel of love flowing from Him. Without divine intervention our condition is terminal. Therefore God sent His Son to restore trust, to remove the fear and doubt from our minds, so that we might freely cooperate with Him for our healing.

We must also remember that even if God's love had previously been flowing through us, if we stop loving and giving ourselves to others our hearts and minds will slowly harden, become increasingly selfish, and ultimately die. We see this, of course, demonstrated in the life of Adam.

Imagine the water flowing through the pipes in your home. The water is pure and clean and abundant from a municipal supply. But what happens to the water in the pipes if you shut off all the spigots and never let the water flow again? Regardless of how pure the water was when it entered your home, it will now stagnate—not because the water supply has shut itself off, but because the spigots are closed, which prevent any more pure water from flowing into your home. Likewise, when we stop loving and giving, we close the heart and mind and isolate ourselves from God's limitless love. It is only by receiving His abundant love and allowing that love to flow through us to others that we grow.

Greater Love

Christ said, "Greater love has no one than this, that he lay down his life for his friends" (John 15:13). Why is sacrificing one's life the greatest love? Because to give one's life to save another is the ultimate end of self-sacrifice. Love is the process of giving, the exact opposite of taking, grasping, or self-seeking. While people may cling to many things, when death comes calling they will gladly surrender all their accumulated possessions to retain their life. When someone is willing to surrender his or her life for another, then there is nothing that he or she will hold back—love has replaced selfishness.

The Ten Commandments and DNA

The principle of selfishness wages war with the principle of love. Self-seeking, self-promotion, and self-exaltation oppose God's methods of love and liberty. God created our planet and humanity in particular as the showcase of His law—His method of running the universe. We can understand the law of love and liberty fully only when we see it at work in an intelligent living being. Reading it on stone will never reveal its true nature. It must be seen in action.

Recently in the news we have heard of legal battles over the display of the Ten Commandments. I have heard some people proclaim that the Ten Commandments are the final word on God's law. But such individuals misunderstand His law. The Ten Commandments are only a transcript of God's law of love and liberty—a dim reflection of its fullness.

The Ten Commandments are like your DNA code. Yes, we can document a person's specific DNA sequence, offering us an accurate transcript of certain aspects of the individual. But would we know the fullness of the person—the sound of laughter, the brightness of a smile, the warmth of his or her love—by studying the DNA code? Likewise, the Ten Commandments are but a dim reflection of God's law of love and liberty. Just studying the Ten Commandments will never reveal the fullness of God's law. Instead, we must see the law in living flesh.

God created humanity to be the repository of His living law of love. It was only after the human race fell and the divine law of love was no longer written in the mind that it became necessary to put it on stone in an attempt to awaken us to our sickly state. But it is God's plan to restore His law of love and liberty in our minds. Regarding the new covenant, the writer of Hebrews, quoting Jeremiah, states, "This is the covenant I will make with the house of Israel after that time, declares the Lord. I will put my laws in their minds and write them on their hearts" (Heb. 8:10).

Brotherly Love

Even though sin mars creation and but dimly reflects the love that exists in the heart of God, we can still see His love displayed in our parents and children, our sisters and brothers, our friends and associates. Often called brotherly love, in human terms it is the closest we see, on a daily basis, to Godlike love. This is because God designed the family to reflect the relationship that exists among the Godhead and between the Godhead and His creation.

Parents are to have a love between them that is so intimate, so close, so private that the two actually come into unity of mind, heart, purpose, disposition, and will. They become trusted and valued confidants and friends. But because of selfishness, even the most harmonious marriage is but a dim reflection of the love and unity among the Godhead.

Outside of the parental unity are the children, the outgrowth and expression of the love of the parents. As the parents' love for each other grows, they join themselves together and share of themselves to create their offspring. This new creation—an outgrowth of their love—becomes the object of their attention and affection.

The parents then devote their resources to the health and welfare of their children. It reflects the constant care of the Father, Son, and Holy Spirit in providing for Their creation. And just as parents will sacrifice themselves to save their child, so too God has sacrificed Himself to save us.

Within the marital relationship God designed the experience of unity to be filled with an abiding peace, constant trust, and intense feelings of joy and pleasure. Yet He never intended such feelings to be an end in themselves, but the beautiful result of self-sacrifice, mutual sharing, rightdoing, and concern for another.

Once Adam failed in his original purpose as the pinnacle of creation—the showpiece for God's law of love and liberty that would reveal to the onlooking universe His methods and principles—there was one more step God could take to reveal Himself and His living law. God became one with us, and in human form He was the repository of His law, demonstrating its height and depth and breadth and endlessness. Christ displayed God's methods of governing the universe. Through His life He revealed God.

Love Heals

God's plan is to take humanity, damaged by sin, born with natural inclinations toward self-seeking, infected with the law of selfishness, and restore in us His law of love and liberty. The Lord does not want simply to put His law in the mind as an idea to be believed, but rather to re-create us in the fullness of His image as living conduits of His love. His law of love will permeate our entire being and become the wellspring of all action. He seeks to elevate us from our fallen state of selfishness with its slavery to fear, insecurity, and feelings, so that we will once again occupy our noble station in God's order. Removing the selfishness from our minds, He will restore in us the living law of love and liberty. Then we will once again stand as intelligent, self-governed, self-sacrificing friends of God—as the living repositories of His great law of love and liberty.

CHAPTER 8

Love's Counterfeits

I wish that when I was younger I had known the truth about the law of love and liberty as described in the previous chapters. It would have helped me to avoid so much heartache and pain. But unfortunately, like most people, I misunderstood love and, therefore, have made some regrettable decisions. Like so many, I had accepted a counterfeit to love and experienced the pain that results when such mistakes are made. To those I have hurt by my failure to love, I am truly sorry. If I could change history and undo the pain I have caused, I would, but this I cannot do. Therefore, I do that which I can: I learn from my mistakes, make right what I am able to, and through God's grace share these truths to help others. In this chapter we are going to explore the counterfeits to love and the common factors that interfere with experiencing the full healing power of God's law of love and liberty.

Love Is Not Controlling

Beep! Beep! Beep! My pager startled me awake. The displayed number was quite familiar to me: the ICU at Hamilton Medical Center, in Dalton, Georgia. After I'd returned the call, the nurse reported that they had just admitted a young man named Jerry, who had tried to kill himself by an overdose of medication. The hospital wanted me to evaluate his further suicide risk.

When I met Jerry, he was lying in a hospital bed with ECG wires running across his chest. An IV in his left forearm was connected to an infusion machine, and the monitor steadily beeped in the background. The charcoal given to neutralize the drugs he had taken blackened his teeth, and dried charcoal was visible on his cheek and where it had dribbled onto his hospital gown. His hair was oily and uncombed, and his face unshaven and unwashed.

After a few minutes of casual conversation to establish a rapport with him, I asked Jerry, "What's going on in your life that brought you to the point of suicide?" Beginning to cry, he told me that his wife was leaving him.

"I want her to come back. I want her to regret leaving and decide to stay. I love her too much to let her go. I told her that if she left me, I would kill myself."

"Why would you try to kill yourself if she no longer wants to be with you?"

"Because I love her."

While Jerry clearly had strong feelings for his wife, his behavior was far from loving. In fact, it violated the law of love and liberty. His focus was not on the health, welfare, and happiness of his wife, but on himself. He was operating from selfishness, not love. If she stayed simply because she feared that he would harm himself if she left, her love for him would die, and resentment would build in its place.

The Word "Love" Has So Many Meanings

True love is difficult to find because of the many counterfeits that masquerade as it. The English language makes this even more difficult because the word "love" has so many meanings and connotations. We "love" our cars, "love" to go to movies, "love" our college football team. This type of "love" is extremely self-centered and could more accurately be called "attachment" or "identification with."

Our passion for such objects or activities derives from self-gratification or self-exaltation. Why do we "love" our Mercedes? Because of how it makes us feel? Because of status? Why do we "love" our college teams? Because we have tied our personal sense of identity and even an aspect of our self-worth to their success. And how do people respond when their teams begin losing? The more they "love" their teams, the more unloving they become. Such "love" is materialistic, self-centered, and fleeting, and obviously not consistent with Godlike love.

Eros

"When desire, having rejected reason and overpowered judgment which leads to right, is set in the direction of the pleasure which beauty can inspire, and when again under the influence of its kindred desires it is moved with violent motion toward the beauty of corporeal forms, it acquires a sur-name from this very violent motion, and is called love" (Socrates).

This form of irrational, emotional, sensual "love" is erotic love. It often succeeds in drawing many victims into its web of destruction. But does true love reject reason and destroy good judgment?

Eroticism counterfeits love in various ways to include pornography, the various perversions, and lust. Erotic "love" is also the basis of adultery, regardless of how passionately "in love" individuals involved in adultery claim to be. True love never damages and destroys, nor does it cheat, lie, or exploit.

While hugely successful at seducing people into participating in it, eroticism, when thought about, is rarely accepted as true love, even by those who practice it. We see this in the fact that most people who indulge in erotic love are, in some way, ashamed of that fact and try to hide it. No father I have met proudly tells his children that he visits strip bars or is ad-dicted to porn videos. Similarly, no mother I have encountered excitedly shares with her children that she has been cheating on their father. No, erotic "love," when thought about, rarely gets confused with true love.

Dependency

But one counterfeit does frequently get mistaken for true love, and, therefore, is the most destructive of all counterfeits. It is so well camou-flaged that many people actually accept it as true love. We know this coun-terfeit as dependency.

What is dependency? A relationship based on a clinging and self-cen-tered need, not on mutual love and respect, it occurs when a person looks to another to be the source and supply of an internal craving such as that of peace, security, confidence, well-being, or self-worth. Basing a relation-ship on such internal need will impair the ability to give, because the per-son seeks such a relationship only in order to satisfy a personal drive.

In dependent relationships, feelings are extremely intense, but typically erratic and unstable. Relationships characterized by dependency are simi-lar to roller coasters, always swinging between extreme ups and downs. Typically, the relationship involves intense attraction and arousal followed by severe irritability and argument, accompanied by few periods of calm.

Because such people are dependent, they want the other individual for internal security or a sense of wellness and so will exert pressure to control them and maintain the relationship. Because such behavior violates free-dom, it will always lead to rebellion. The dependent party experiences the rebellion as threatened abandonment or loss, and the insecurity increases, leading to an even greater need to hold on and control. The result is a vicious downward spiral.

Jerry's marriage was just such a relationship, one characterized by intense feelings of attraction and need followed by manipulation and control, with the inevitable disintegration of self when the relationship failed.

Dependency Is Like a Navy Diver

Imagine the case of a navy diver, the old-fashioned type depicted in the movie *Men of Honor,* starring Cuba Gooding, Jr., and Robert De Niro. In that movie they wore suits with air lines to the surface, where pumps delivered air to the divers below. If you were one of those men, you would be dependent on those on the surface for your air. Should someone on the surface tell you to stand on one foot or they would cut off your air, what would you do? And if you wanted to go to the right, but the ship turned to the left, what choice would you have? It parallels the situation in a dependent relationship, in which true freedom does not exist. But because the need is so great, intense feelings get associated with the one toward whom the dependence is directed.

Imagine yourself drowning underwater and then someone bringing you an air line. Would you value that person? Would you have intense feelings for the individual? Would you want to hold on to him or her? And how would it feel if he or she decided to leave and take the air line away?

Individuals can become so dependent on the emotional support from those on whom they rely that they experience the threat of losing their source of nurturance with the same fear and anxiety that divers would if someone threatened to cut their air off. It feels as if they are going to die. Because their anxiety is so intense, persons in dependent relationships go to extremes and take desperate measures to prove their "love" to the ones on whom they depend in order to convince them to stay. And if the proclamations of affection don't get returned, often the dependent persons will threaten harm to themselves or even those on whom they cling—all designed to retain control of the needed person.

It was the situation that Jerry found himself in. He clung to his wife for a sense of well-being. Without her, the sense of emptiness and of individual disintegration became so great that he was willing to risk his life in an attempt to maintain control of her. But if Jerry's wife were to stay because of his threat to kill himself, she would lose her freedom and become a hostage to his threats. Eventually she would develop resentment and rebellion, and the marriage would be doomed to failure.

Dependency Is Like Siamese Twins

Consider Siamese twins attached at the hip. People growing up in this condition come to consider it as normal. Throughout the life of the Siamese twins there exists a constant struggle for control, as neither can function without the other. They often meet the suggestion of separation with fear and insecurity, as neither has ever functioned on their own. Each feels that they will lose part of themselves, when in reality they are losing only the unhealthy attachment to the other. The actual process of separation is painful yet not destructive, and it actually results in individual healing and increased autonomy.

Those in dependent relationships experience many of the same symptoms. Attempting to break the unhealthy attachments often feels as if they are losing part of themselves, and often results in resistance to separating. When unhealthy attachments have solidified, cutting them is often painful. But severing unhealthy attachments does not mean losing the other person, just the dependency with its associated baggage of control.

In the case of the Siamese twins, following the separation they can continue to spend time together, but now it will be because they *freely choose* to, not because they *have* to. And after breaking the unhealthy connection, the Siamese twins can now participate in far more activities than they were able to enjoy when joined. They can ride a tandem bicycle, play hide-and-seek, play catch, and so much more. Likewise, when a relationship rids itself of dependency, it can grow, as individuals are able to engage in so many more healthy experiences.

The Origins of Dependency

How does dependency get started? All children have a natural, God-given longing to be loved and accepted by their parents. It is a reflection of the love and trust we are to have with our heavenly Father. But all children are also born infected with selfishness, which distorts and impairs healthy love from being experienced and expressed.

Depending on a multiplicity of factors that include parenting, the temperament of the child, the environment, the child's biological makeup, and the freewill choices of the child and spiritual upbringing, the infecting element of selfishness can grow increasingly stronger, and healthy love may never take root. Parents have the primary responsibility to raise their children in ways that will instill healthy love and eradicate selfishness. Unfortunately, this doesn't always happen. When healthy love does not successfully emerge and instead selfishness dominates, dependency is frequently the result.

Before I go on, I want to clarify for those who may be struggling with rebellious children what the responsibilities of parenting are. Parents are *not* responsible for the *outcomes* of their children's lives. But they *are* accountable for their conduct in parenting. Because children have free will and because there exist many influences other than parental ones, parents are never responsible for outcomes. But parents are always accountable for their own decisions and actions.

This said, however, parental influence is significant and must be taken seriously. Unhealthy parenting will injure children, making it more difficult for them to develop healthy characters. But even when parenting is not only unhealthy but overtly abusive, the child can experience healing from the injuries of the abuse and ultimately become whole. Healthy parenting does not guarantee a good outcome, but provides significant advantages toward such a goal. Likewise, unhealthy parenting does not guarantee a bad outcome, but creates disadvantages that make a favorable outcome more difficult.

All children desire parental approval and validation. In dysfunctional families, however, the desire for affirmation from the parents does not get gratified in healthy ways. The basic dysfunction is unopposed selfishness in the parent that results in the parents seeking to get parental needs met from the child, rather than seeking to sacrifice themselves to meet the needs of the child. An unhealthy parent sends mixed signals of approval/disapproval, triggering insecurity in the child. The conflicting signals cause the child to fail to develop a healthy internal sense of self, and instead train the child to continue to look to the parents for external validation. This results in an overly intense longing for love, affirmation, and acceptance.

The child spends his or her energy seeking nurturance from the parent, and the parent uses the child's longing as a constant source of control and manipulation. The child grows to have an ever-increasing ambivalence toward the parent. Intense longing for parental approval alternates with resentment and anger. The destructive and hostile feelings toward the parent then lead to guilt. The guilt is accompanied by the fear that, if the feelings of anger and resentment should be acted on, the child will lose his or her parent and then never get the affirmation so desperately craved.

In unhealthy families, unfortunately, the children never receive the affirmation they seek. Young children idealize their parents. It means that they see their parents as nearly perfect, with almost supernatural abilities. Therefore, when parental rejection occurs, the child makes the only conclusion he or she can: "If my parent is perfect and if I am unaccepted, something must be wrong with me." The child is incapable of recognizing that the parent is the actual problem.

Imagine walking out of your local supermarket and seeing in the parking lot a 50-year-old man cursing a 5-year-old girl. He is calling her every foul name that you have ever heard. Do you immediately think, *What a terrible 5-year-old girl?* No! You instantly recognize that the man has problems. But what does the little girl walk away feeling like? What does she think? And what if the man was her father? Too many people go through life like the 5-year-old girl. Whenever someone treats them badly, they believe that something is wrong with them. Recall the woman in the preface of this book—this was one of Her problems. Not only did someone call Her bad names, but he treated Her in vile ways. She never realized that the problem was not with Her but with the man who was abusing Her.

This template of relating to self and to others gets established in dysfunctional families before children develop the mental ability to be introspective and reason such things out. Therefore, they operate within this perspective without even becoming aware of the problem. Dysfunctional family life trains children to depend on another's opinion or feedback as the barometer to measure their worth. They unconsciously accept the false belief that the opinions of others are more important than the truth.

Children in such situations feel as if they are incomplete in some way and will go to great lengths to obtain the affirmation they so desperately seek, but they never get it from others and never will. No matter how wonderful the external validation, it never satisfies, because they have formed an identity based on the inconsistent experiences of childhood. Unfortunately, such children usually fail to recognize that the problem is not in themselves but in their chaotic upbringing. As a result they remain trapped in a distorted self-image.

Dependency Is Like Trying to Get Milk From a Bull

Consider visiting a farm and going out each morning to get milk from a bull. It doesn't matter how desperately you want milk; the bull can't give you something it doesn't have. But let's say you don't know anything about farms and don't realize that bulls don't produce milk. You might conclude that your inexperience is causing the problem, so you go back day after day seeking the milk.

The continued lack of success frustrates you. Suddenly you find an explanation for your failure: you recall reading that bulls don't like red. You realize that you've worn your red bandanna each time you sought milk from the bull, so now you begin to dress in other colors. Still no milk.

Next you remember that animals like music, so you bring a stereo with you and play a variety of songs, but still no milk. At times you beg the bull, but with no results. Bringing special food, you hope that a change in diet will produce milk, but again to no avail.

By now you have become not only frustrated but angry. Briefly you consider shooting the bull, but as the thought of doing so runs through your mind, an explosion of feelings, like a train whistle, screams from within: *If I do that, I'll never get the milk.* And then you feel terrible guilt and begin the process all over again.

What is the problem in this scenario? Failure to see the truth: Bulls don't give milk! Many of my patients have a difficult time accepting the reality that they have parents incapable of giving them the affirmation, love, and acceptance they need. It leaves them continually vulnerable to the manipulations of their parents, and constantly and chronically insecure as they continue to believe that the problem centers within them.

Imagine in our bull example that the bull is intelligent. Is it possible that because the bull enjoys the attention and special treatment, he might lead you to believe that one day—if you keep it up—you just might get some milk? Unfortunately, many human beings are like that. While so self-centered that they are incapable of providing nurturance to others, they still enjoy the attention they get from others trying for their approval, so they lead the dependent party to assume that one day they just might receive the love and affirmation desired.

Back on the farm, you finally recognize that bulls don't give milk. Does that mean you can never have anything to do with the bull? Of course not. You can still have the bull pull a plow or cart. The difference is that because you don't need something from it, you aren't held hostage by the animal. You can now come and go freely.

Dependency Makes It Difficult to Tolerate the Anger of Others

When we care about someone, it is difficult to set boundaries and say no, especially when we know that the other person will be unhappy with us for doing so. Encountering the anger of others is extremely uncomfortable, even when we are doing what is healthy. This is especially true when our parents have conditioned us to need their dysfunctional approval. Ignoring the problem might seem easier than confronting the situation. But the consequences are often far worse. Because the problem continues to build, by the time it finally gets addressed it is usually much larger.

Dependency is a hopelessly destructive cycle, as such behavior violates God's law of love and liberty. The unfortunate result is greater loss of self-esteem, self-worth, and self-confidence accompanied by an ever-increasing need for further external validation. Therefore, individuals caught up in it continue to be empty buckets seeking to be filled by the emotional support of others. But because they are unable to retain that support, they never experience real stability or wellness. Those in the nurturing role eventually become exhausted, reach their limits, and can give no more. The dependent person then interprets this loss of nurturance as rejection and responds with overwhelming hostility and anger. Such is dependency, the great counterfeit to love.

True Love Is Not Natural

When I ask my patients how to tell what true love is, far too many respond by saying, "By the way it feels." But as we have already discovered, feelings are entirely unreliable and can often deceive. Many of us, for example, have experienced the confusion of thinking we are in love only to later discover that we've been mistaken.

Human beings do not naturally possess true love. It is a love quite the opposite of our natural desires, of selfishness, of our genetic inheritance, of egotism, and of the id. True love is the principle of doing what's in the best interest of the other person, the principle of giving—of beneficence, regardless of how one might actually feel.

Parents, do you remember taking your toddler to get vaccines? Did it feel good for you or your child? Then why did you do it? Because your reason and conscience recognized it was in your child's best interest to get the vaccines. And because you love your child, you chose to have someone stick a needle in your child even though it caused pain. But the pain was not what was intended—it was something unavoidable in order to get the vaccine.

Do you think you took any risks that your toddler might not understand? From the child's perspective, what do you imagine it was like to get vaccinated? "Mommy, Daddy, why are you doing this? Why are you letting them hurt me? Don't you love me?"

But because you love your children, were you willing to be misunderstood in order to do what you knew was best for them, even when it felt bad? That is how love works. Sometimes it feels good, while other times it hurts. But love always heals, always protects, always builds up, never destroys, never seeks its own. True love is not motivated by feelings.

Love Does What Is Right

Think of Christ in the Garden of Gethsemane. He was about to experience the cross, the greatest act of love ever known in all history, and what were His feelings? He was in anguish. He agonized. He suffered (see Matt. 26:36-44; Mark 14:32-42; Luke 22:39-46). If Christ had based His actions on how He felt, He would not have gone through with the cross. Love is not a feeling, but an action in spite of feelings.

When we love others, we will be willing to risk being misunderstood in order to do what is in their best interest. God did this all through the Old Testament. Many times He raised His voice to get the attention of His unruly children, because He loved them and didn't want them to destroy themselves. Yet consider the risks He took. Many might conclude that God is a severe, vengeful, arbitrary being who requires some kind of appeasement. In fact, many have decided that God was exactly like that. But love does what is right and reasonable because it is right and reasonable, not because of what others will think.

True love stems from knowing God. When we know Him, as it is our privilege, we find our hearts broken in admiration and adoration for the great sacrifice He has made to reach us. The recognition of the immense measures He took upon Himself leads to gratitude in our hearts. As we learn to know Him, we come to love, admire, respect, and trust Him. We learn His methods and principles, and then we begin to practice them in our own lives. Our desire to stand for what is true and healthy eventually outweighs our concern for ourselves, and we begin to walk on a higher plane of existence, free from fear and insecurity. God re-creates us within and endows us with a power outside of ourselves that enables our continued advancement and growth.

Love Is the Opposite of Dependency

Love heals, while dependency destroys. Love liberates, while dependency always seeks to control. Love gives, while dependency constantly takes. Love is fearless, while dependency is fear-ridden. Love is interested in another, while dependency focuses on self. Love is stable, while dependency wavers. Love is orderly and reliable, while dependency is chaotic and unreliable. Love is based on principle, while dependency is based on feelings. Love is consistent, while dependency is inconsistent. Love is honest and truthful, while dependency is dishonest and deceitful. Love is patient, while dependency is impulsive. Love is kind, while dependency is cruel. Love is forgiving, while dependency is resentful. Love protects, while dependency exploits. Love sacrifices self, while dependency sacrifices others. Love never ends, while dependency never lasts. And love never fails, while dependency never succeeds.

CHAPTER 9

Faith—Fact or Fiction?

*"It is useless to tell one not to reason but to believe—
you might as well tell a man not to wake
but sleep."—Lord Byron.*

O ne of the first aims of psychotherapy is to develop a working rapport, a therapeutic alliance, with the patient. Without trust, confidence, and faith in the doctor, the patient will not put into practice the treatment plan that seeks to bring healing. The same is also true in God's plan to heal us. Without a therapeutic alliance—without trust or faith in God—we will not apply to our lives His plan to heal. Therefore, He has gone to great lengths to help us build trust and faith in Him. So what exactly is faith, where does it come from, and how does it work?

I Know That I Know!

A famous televangelist passionately told his enthusiastic and emotionally supportive audience, "I know that I know that I know that I know." As I watched from the comforts of my living room, I thought, *How does he know?* Hoping to discover the source of what he so confidently proclaimed, I continued watching. Unfortunately, he never explained it. He just proclaimed that he knew.

The televangelist professed to have faith, but he didn't clearly explore its foundation or reveal its source. The way he approached faith reminded me of the little boy's explanation: "Faith is believing what you know ain't so." Is this really the essence of faith?

Recently I attended a local high school graduation during which one of the honor students recounted how her faith had been integral in helping her succeed in her young career. During her speech she quoted H. L. Mencken: "Faith may be defined briefly as an illogical belief in the occurrence of the improbable." It sounded again very much like the little boy's definition of faith. Does faith really involve believing in something with-out evidence, believing in things that don't make sense? Does faith really require that you convince yourself that something is true even though your best judgment says otherwise?

I Know You'll Be Just Fine

Imagine that you have been sick for several days with a variety of symp-toms—high fever, productive cough, chills and sweats, muscle aches, a crack-ling sound in your chest when you breathe deeply—so you go to a nearby emergency room. To your relief, you discover that the attending physician is a Christian. Your encouragement rises further after you disclose your symp-toms and the ER physician walks across the room, bows his head, and prays. But your heart sinks when he returns and says, "I've heard everything you have to say, but after praying, I have a really good feeling inside that there is nothing wrong. You go on home. I know you'll be just fine."

What would you do? Would you ask, "How do you know I'll be fine?" Suppose he answered, "I know that I know that I know." Would that be sufficient? Would you now return home? Or would you want a second opinion?

Soon another doctor arrives, listens to your history, and checks your temperature, heart rate, and blood pressure. Pulling out his stethoscope, he listens to your lungs, orders lab work, evaluates your blood count, and then requests a chest X-ray that he carefully reviews. After obtaining and eval-uating all this evidence, he draws a conclusion: You have pneumonia.

When the second doctor tells you his diagnosis—based on extensive evidence—do you get a *feeling* of conviction, a *feeling* of confidence, a *feel-ing* of certainty, a *feeling* of faith that he is right? Is the *feeling* the evidence, or is it a *result* of the evidence?

The feeling of conviction emerges as the mind comes to understand truth. As the understanding of the truth increases, so does one's confidence and faith.

Most of us share a similar reaction in such circumstances. When the doctor tells us the diagnosis, and we recognize that it's true, we experience a sensation of confidence—of faith. Great relief sweeps over us. It feels good—so good, in fact, that many people innocently accept the feeling as truth. But it's not!

Biblical Evidence or Powerful Feelings?

During my residency one of the interns on my team had extremely strong religious convictions. Although he and I did not share identical be-liefs, we spent many hours discussing our different points of view. Early in our acquaintance, before we had shared many details about our religious backgrounds, he told me that he believed in the King James Version of the Bible. Because of this encouraging insight, I thought that we would have a great time studying together. Naively I thought that with thorough Bible study that would give us solid biblical evidence, we would soon enjoy a closer religious fellowship. Unfortunately, it did not happen.

During our studies he often demonstrated excitement about a new in-sight, only to return the next day to reverse himself completely and reclaim confidence in his previously held position. Surprisingly, he never offered any fresh support.

Not long afterward I discovered why biblical evidence had such little impact on him. His method for determining truth rested on a key passage from a nineteenth-century writer: "And when ye shall receive these things, I would exhort you that ye would ask God, the Eternal Father, in the name of Christ, if these things are not true; and if ye shall ask with a sincere heart, with real intent, having faith in Christ, he will manifest the truth of it unto you, by the power of the Holy Ghost. And by the power of the Holy Ghost ye may know the truth of all things."[1]

While it sounds wonderful at first reading, my colleague had inter-preted it in this way: If you want to know whether something is true or not, you don't need to search for evidence, examine that evidence with your God-given reasoning powers, and compare it with previous revela-tion. Instead, go to your prayer closet and pray to God for an impression, a feeling of conviction to tell you whether something is true or not.

This conclusion is similar to that held by the first doctor in the emer-gency room scenario I presented earlier in this chapter. Recall that he had "a really good feeling inside that there is nothing wrong" in spite of the obvious symptoms. The feeling of conviction was more important than the evidence. In fact, the feeling of conviction got accepted as supreme evi-dence that superseded all other evidence.

However, James 1:13, 14 cautions us against such subjectivity by pointing out its potential danger in another area: "When tempted, no one should say, 'God is tempting me.' For God cannot be tempted by evil, nor does he tempt anyone; but each one is tempted when, by his own evil de-sire [or feelings], he is dragged away and enticed."

Evil has no truth on its side. Therefore, Satan uses whatever strategy he can to persuade people to set aside their reliance on truth. My intern friend isn't the only one who substitutes feelings for truth. Many well-meaning Christians act in an identical manner, when, instead of implementing truth understood, they wait for some internal feeling before acting.

The Road to Emmaus

After Christ's resurrection two disciples who were walking on the road to Emmaus were joined by a stranger, who we know was Christ. They were discouraged because of the Crucifixion. How did Christ deal with them? Did He perform a miraculous sign and declare that He was the risen Savior? No! Instead He took them through the Bible, revealing to them the biblical evidence confirming who He was and what His mission was. Not until they were convinced by the weight of biblical evidence did He reveal His identity. And as He opened the scriptural evidence to them, their hearts burned within them (Luke 24:13-32). In other words, the evidence resulted in a change in feelings. Again, though, the feelings were not evidence. Why is this important? Because anyone can make claims, but the truth will support only those who are truthful.

Bill Clinton stood before the nation and proclaimed that he had not had sexual relations with Monica Lewinsky. But when she brought forth her dress, the evidence exposed his deception. Likewise, Satan has claims, but God has the truth, so He doesn't need, nor does He desire, that we believe because of His personal declarations. If we follow truth, we always find God. As Christ said: "The truth will set you free" (John 8:32).

Faith Is the Substance of Things Hoped For

Consider Hebrews 11:1, which states, "Faith is the substance of things hoped for, the evidence of things not seen" (KJV). Doesn't this mean we are to believe even though it doesn't make sense or we don't have evidence?

The English translation of this text uses the word "substance," a Latin-based word derived from the Greek *hypostasis*. Let's do a little word sleuthing and discover what the words mean in English. *Hypostasis* has two parts, the first being *hypo,* meaning "low" or "under," as in *hypo*glycemic (low blood sugar) or *hypo*tension (low blood pressure) or *hypo*dermic injection (under the dermis/skin). The second part, *stasis,* means "standing" or "standstill." Hypostasis was translated into Latin as "substance." The first part of the word, *sub,* indicates "under," as in *sub*way or *sub*terranean or *sub*marine, and the latter part, *stance,* means "standing." With this insight, then, we could offer a modern translation of the passage as: "Faith is our *under-stand-ing* of things hoped for, the evidence of things not seen." The more understanding you have, the more faith you have.

Imagine you are the parent of a first grader. While your child is at school, you buy a present, wrap it, and place it in your bedroom closet. When your child gets home, you tell her to go to your closet because you have a present there waiting for her. Does your child go? If so, does she do so based on the substance (understanding) of the present not yet received? No! Does your child head for the closet based on the evidence of the present not yet seen? No! Well, then, why does the child run to the closet? Because of faith in you. While your child has no understanding or evidence of the present, she has overwhelming understanding and evidence of your honesty, reliability, and trustworthiness.

The presents in our heavenly closet are eternal life, a crown of glory, mansions in heaven, and much more. We have no physical evidence for their existence, but we have overwhelming understanding and evidence for the existence of God and His reliability, trustworthiness, and goodness. Our faith in God, therefore, is based not on feelings, wishful thinking, or impressions, but on *solid evidences revealed both in nature and in God's Written Word* (see Rom. 1:20).

As your child walks down the hall to find the present, does she hesitate from a sense of fear and uncertainty, wondering whether the closet really contains anything? Or does she go skipping gleefully down the hall, already experiencing the joy of the present while still on the way to find it? This is to be the Christian experience, already experiencing the joy of our heavenly presents because the One who has promised them is reliable.

The God Beyond the Sky

A recent Bible study guide included the following thought:

"There is always the need for faith, which is belief in something we don't totally see or understand. If we could totally see it or understand it, then there would be no room for faith. We don't need faith to believe that the sky is over our heads. We can look up and see it. Faith is needed, instead, to believe in the God who lives beyond that sky, because we can't see Him." [2]

If this is the correct understanding of faith, do you think that when you get to heaven and meet God face to face, you will say, "Lord, I used to have faith in You, but now that I can see You, I don't have faith in You anymore"? Or will your faith be a million times stronger?

The danger in believing without evidence, of accepting things on emotional feelings, is that it opens one up to believe anything. In addition, if we measure the strength of our faith by our feelings, then as our feelings rise and fall, so will our estimation of our level of faith. We will judge God's presence by our inconsistent feelings and conclude that sometimes He is near and other times He's not.

Truth Always Supports God

In this conflict between good and evil, truth always supports God and always refutes Satan. Therefore, Satan must persuade people to believe without valuing the truth or exploring its evidence. He is even happier if he can totally destroy the mental faculties of reason and conscience, the avenues through which truth enters the mind. Without reason and conscience, we are unable to distinguish the true from the false.

Spiritualism—A Counterfeit of Faith

Spiritualism is one of Satan's greatest successes in counterfeiting true faith and the working of the Spirit of God. As we discovered in earlier chapters, the Spirit of God operates by revealing truth to our minds in ways that we can comprehend, and then leaves us free to reach our own conclusions. When we decide to follow the truth, we receive divine power sufficient for the task. By this method God constantly strengthens and ennobles the spiritual nature—reason and conscience—and the individual develops ever-increasing discernment and wisdom. The character is purified, while stability and self-control are established.

Spiritualism, however, is the great counterfeit of the working of the Spirit of God that, rather than healing the mind, slowly destroys our reason and conscience. It is so subtle that it enters many Christian circles without notice. Many people worry about spiritualism, but they don't know how to identify it.

One common thread runs through all forms of spiritualism, whether it is witchcraft, Wicca, tarot cards, voodoo, black magic, wizardry, astrology, or anything else. If you want to identify spiritualism, look for this thread, and you will see it no matter how it is disguised. *Spiritualism is the pursuit of knowledge without the use of reason and the investigation of evidence.*

Because the truth refutes Satan, his only hope for success is to convince people to value things other than truth and evidence. Therefore, Satan urges people to search for knowledge without evidence and without depending on reason. This results in the gradual destruction of the image of God within. People become superstitious, fearful, and uncertain because reason fades as people transfer their faith to things that don't make sense.

The loss of reason results in immature Christians tossed about by every doctrinal fad. It is only by exercising reason in the examination of evidence that Christians grow into full maturity, learning to discern the true from the false. Truth both sets us free and heals.

Faith Is Not Dependent on Miracles

Satan also depends on miraculous signs and wonders to distract the mind. Consider Eve in the garden, where she experienced the miracle of a serpent speaking, yet the miracle did not prove that what the serpent said was true.

Imagine yourself in a church board meeting when the discussion turns to two views on baptism. As one person rises, claiming that he will prove that the Holy Spirit endorses his position, he approaches another board member plagued by polio since childhood. When he shouts, "In the name of the Lord, walk," the polio victim does indeed stand and begin to stroll about the room. Does it prove the board member's position is right? No! Miracles can be counterfeited. The truth is the truth regardless of accompanying signs and wonders. Satan has no truth, but he is a supernatural being who can fascinate the human race with certain miracles, which will deceive those who have not learned the value of relying on truth alone.

Faith Is Integral in Healing the Mind

Faith is the hand that reaches out and takes hold of the hand of God. As such, faith is integral for healing of the mind. In order for faith to be healing, however, it must be evidence-based, truth-based, and fact-based. While feelings can accompany faith, they never determine it. Truth establishes faith. Consequently, as our understanding of truth increases, so will our faith.

Spiritualism, on the other hand, is a counterfeit to genuine faith and, as we have already noted, involves the pursuit of knowledge without the use of reason or the investigation of evidence. It sacrifices evidence for emotional highs and miraculous signs. Miraculous signs and wonders do not establish faith, because they can be counterfeited. As we have already stated, the truth is the truth regardless of whether or not it has accompanying miracles.

When I think of my patient in the preface, I remember how angry She would get when people asked Her to trust them. She became especially furious when someone told Her to trust God. I believe that She would have been comfortable with the realization that trust in God is based on evidence that appeals to the reason. As a result She would have liked a God who never demands that we just trust Him, but simply goes about being trustworthy and inviting us to get to know Him and decide for ourselves. Will She ever know?

---

[1] Moroni 10:4, 5, *The Book of Mormon.*
[2] "Bible Biographies, Actors in the Drama Called *Planet Earth,*" *Adult Bible Study Guide,* April-June 2001, p. 90.

CHAPTER 10

Restoring Order

In her 20s, Jane was an attractive blond with a slim build and blue eyes that seemed to emit a light of their own. She had grown up in a fairly typical middle-class home, with two siblings, cat and dog, and both parents at home. Although she had suffered no abuse, as the middle child she often felt neglected. Regardless of her excellent grades, her model behavior, or her numerous awards at school, she concluded that she just wasn't good enough. Now in her early adult years Jane struggled with chronic feelings of worthlessness.

One of the most common problems facing many of my patients is that sense of worthlessness. To help us understand how to cope with powerful feelings, let's take this example and examine it in light of our understanding of God's hierarchy of the mind.

The greatest mistake people make when dealing with difficult feelings is that of accepting them as true. When most people feel worthless, they allow the feeling to take control of their thoughts and then imagine themselves in humiliating or demoralizing situations. The thoughts begin to follow the influence of this feeling, and a torrent of negative ideas rushes through their minds: "How could I be so stupid?" "You ugly good-for-nothing, what made you think he would ever go out with you?" "You can't do anything right. Why bother?"

Such negative ideas reinforce the feeling of worthlessness, which, when nurtured, matures into a well-entrenched false belief. With this false belief firmly ingrained, the mind begins to filter experiences through it. Experiences that support the distorted self-image get replayed repeatedly, further strengthening the feeling and belief of worthlessness. Meanwhile, the mind discounts and rejects positive experiences that should refute the false belief. Jane was living in such self-imposed mental anguish. She felt trapped and didn't know how to find her way out.

How Do You Know Your Worth?

Christ said, "The truth will set you free" (John 8:32). When my patients disclose that they feel worthless, I pose a few questions that lead them to confront the situation: "Are you really worthless? Are you really worth absolutely nothing?" Regardless of the answer, I ask yet another question: "How do you know?" This raises the issue that applies to *all* feelings: How can you tell whether a feeling is telling the truth or not? Because feelings can lie, how can you determine whether they are accurate or not when they all seem so real? I raise such questions in an attempt to stimulate reason to become involved in this mental conflict. Because truth enters the mind through the reason, it is essential to utilize approaches that will strengthen this mental faculty.

Consider this situation: A person dressed in a dark suit and wearing dark glasses knocks on your door. When you open the door, he demands, "Let me in. I'm from the FBI." What would you do? Would you ask for identification, or would you simply allow him to enter? Why do you want identification? Because you want evidence to verify his claim. Exactly the same thing must happen when a feeling knocks on the door to your mind: Elevate the feeling to reason and conscience, and ask for evidence to verify or refute its validity.

Let's return to the feeling of worthlessness. What evidence do we have for such a conclusion? On the most fundamental level, the constituent chemicals in our bodies are worth approximately $25. Many people can sell their blood plasma for $30 each week. How much do people pay for your services at work? How much did you and others invest in your education? Such simple examples provide minor evidence that the feeling of worthlessness is not accurate. But the most powerful support of our worth comes when we ask, "Who is Jesus Christ?" The Son of God. "How much is He worth?" Everything. Priceless. "Did He, or did He not, give His life for you?" Yes, He did!

This is evidence, not mere claims! Jesus didn't simply proclaim how much you're worth. He gave evidence—He sacrificed His life. Now your reason and conscience recognize the evidence demonstrating your great worth, but your feelings continue to inform you that you're worthless. And right in the middle, between the two, is the will. You have to decide. Which will you choose to believe: the evidence or your feelings?

Everything Depends on the Right Action of the Will

It is imperative to recognize the importance of the will. Everything depends on the right action of the will because it is the part of mind that chooses. Consider when Satan took Christ to the pinnacle of the Temple. The devil tempted Him to throw Himself off from there. Satan could not push Christ off—Christ had to make the decision Himself. The same thing applies to our own conflict with Satan. He can never force the will. Rather, we must *choose* to surrender ourselves to his suggestions. This is true even when the temptation comes from within. The book of James tells us that when we find ourselves tempted, "no one should say, 'God is tempting me.' For God cannot be tempted by evil, nor does he tempt anyone; but each one is tempted when, by his own evil desire, he is dragged away and enticed. Then, after desire has conceived, it gives birth to sin; and sin, when it is full-grown, gives birth to death" (James 1:13-15).

James here describes the power of the will. It is only after the internal desire is conceived that it becomes sinful [destructive]. The conception of the desire occurs when the will chooses the desire—when the will says yes to it. It does not matter whether or not you actually carry out the action. If the will says yes, but you never perform the act, the mind is still damaged, the conscience bruised, and the reason clouded.

Imagine that while you're standing at the grocery checkout, the cashier turns away to attend to something. As you look down and see the cash register door open, a thought runs through your mind: *I could sure use that money.* In a flash you decide to reach out and grab a handful. But just as your arm responds to your brain's instructions, the cashier returns to her post, so you abruptly cancel your intention and take nothing.

What happens in your mind? Because you made the choice to steal, you have nudged your character one degree toward that of a thief, even though actions never completed the thought. It will be more difficult to resist such a temptation next time. If the process repeats itself long enough, one eventually loses the ability to discern the right from the wrong; the healthy from the unhealthy. Reason and conscience slowly get destroyed.

Feelings Don't Just Evaporate

Let's return to our discussion of worthlessness. Choosing to believe the evidence does not cause the sense of worthlessness to evaporate immediately. But it does allow Jane to deal with it from a position of confidence and strength. She can have certainty that she is worthwhile even though she may feel worthless at the moment, thus avoiding despondency and hopelessness. After recognizing her worth, she could then take the next step in evaluating where the inaccurate feeling of worthlessness originated.

Motioning toward my office window, I pointed out the hills in the distance and asked her, "If a flare burst off over those hills, and I asked you what is going on over there, what would you say?"

"I don't know," she replied. "I would have to go and look." Exactly! Feelings are like psychological flares. They go off and tell us something is happening in a certain direction, but we don't know what until we investigate. If a flare went off above the hills to the east of my office, while we wouldn't know the cause, we would know that it wasn't something to the west, south, or north. Whatever the problem, it was happening to the east.

When a feeling of worthlessness enters someone's mind, they know, through a review of the evidence, that it is not a conclusion based on actual worthlessness. With great certainty they realize that the evidence reveals their true worth. They also recognize that whatever feeling is masquerading as worthlessness is coming, not from a source of positive feelings (such as happiness, joy, elation, or romance), but from something negative and unpleasant. And this is where each individual begins to uncover their own unique issues that give rise to the sensation of worthlessness, whether it is rejection from a boyfriend or girlfriend who just broke up with them, or from a sense of failure that accompanies divorce.

Elevating feelings to reason and conscience for examination and investigation in light of the facts, evidence, and truth, and then choosing to follow that truth will always restore order and bring peace to the mind. The greatest battle is learning to value truth because it *is* true, not just because it *feels* true.

These Diamonds Are Worthless

In Jane's case she discovered she was feeling worthless because she had never experienced that her parents valued her. She believed that they were disappointed in her. Jane drew her conclusions from her estimation of her parents' opinion, not from reality itself.

To help her recognize her situation, I asked her to imagine that I had presented her parents with a handful of diamonds worth more than $1 million. Surprised, her parents had glanced at the diamonds and exclaimed, "This is ridiculous. No one would give away diamonds. These are nothing but cut glass." So they threw the gemstones into the trash can. With this scenario in Jane's mind, I posed this question: "Simply because your parents thought the diamonds were worthless, does that make them worthless?" When she said no, I looked at her and said, "You're the diamond! Your parents' opinion doesn't change your value!"

Then I proposed something else for her to consider. I asked her if a $100 bill that I handed her would have any value or worth. "Yes," she replied. What if I crumpled it into a wad—would it be worth any less? She shook her head. Suppose I threw it on the floor, stomped on it, and got mud on it; would it be worth any less? Again she answered no. Then I said, "That's you. It doesn't matter if you have been crumpled, stomped on, or gotten dirty in this life. Your worth hasn't changed."

Feelings are extremely unreliable and will lead into destructive avenues if not first confirmed or rejected through a reasonable evaluation of the evidence.

Let's explore one other feeling: guilt. Guilt is destructive and often mishandled because there are two types of guilt—legitimate and illegitimate.

Legitimate Guilt

Legitimate guilt occurs when we do something wrong—something out of harmony with the law of love and liberty, such as stealing from our neighbor. It is a sense of conviction or self-judgment that results from the Holy Spirit directly impressing our conscience and from our own evaluation about our behavior. The way we resolve legitimate guilt is by repentance (a change of heart, not simple confession) and restoration. If you experience guilt after stealing $50 from your neighbor, the only way to resolve it is by repenting and then going to your neighbor and paying back what you took.

Illegitimate Guilt—Type I

The problem with illegitimate guilt is that repentance and restoration do not resolve it, because there is nothing to repent or restore. But because illegitimate guilt *feels* just like legitimate guilt, most people try to deal with illegitimate guilt the same way they would legitimate forms of it. But not only does it not work; it actually makes matters worse.

As an example, illegitimate guilt occurs when a wife comes home from work to find her husband in a bad mood. As he gripes and complains, the wife feels guilty and tries to make amends through repentance and restoration—even though she has done nothing to cause her husband's behavior. "I'm sorry; what can I do?" But her response never works, because she has done nothing for which she needs to repent and she has no ability to restore what she hasn't taken.

Attempting to handle illegitimate guilt in this way always delays resolution of the problem. By accepting illegitimate guilt and trying to repent and restore, one accepts and supports a lie, a falsehood, that would, in the case above, allow the husband to blame his inappropriate behavior on the wife. Instead of the husband recognizing his rudeness to his spouse, taking responsibility for it, and making amends, the wife assumes responsibility for the husband's bad mood. Such a response never resolves the situation, but in fact violates the law of liberty, as the wife is held hostage by the husband's moods.

The way to handle illegitimate guilt is by confronting the truth. Step back and ask yourself, "Did I do anything wrong or inappropriate?" Then recognize the truth and apply the law of liberty. "I didn't do anything wrong. I'm sorry my husband is in a bad mood; if he needs to brood, he's free to do so. I'll empathize, let him know I love him, but not take responsibility to fix it. He is accountable for his own moods."

We must be prepared to let others pout, cry, or be hurt, angry, or upset without apologizing or attempting to fix it if, in truth, no wrong has been done. The imposition of illegitimate guilt is an all-too-common violation of the law of liberty utilized by some as a way to manipulate and control others. It is by using reason and conscience to evaluate the evidence and apply the truth that one avoids being trapped by such feelings.

Illegitimate Guilt—Type II

Let's consider yet another source of illegitimate guilt, one that is very subtle, quite damaging, and far too common.

At the Veterans Affairs Medical Center in Augusta, Georgia, I first met Jeff after his primary-care physician admitted him to the medical-surgical ward to evaluate the man's chronic weight loss, nausea, and abdominal pain. His physical symptoms were a result of years of heavy alcohol use. Jeff had been drinking for nearly 30 years in an attempt to forget the past and avoid chronic feelings of guilt. But no matter how much he drank, the guilt persisted.

As a pilot during the Vietnam War, Jeff had participated in many missions and no doubt had killed numerous enemy soldiers. Because he knew he was saving the lives of his fellow soldiers, he never experienced guilt for the enemy deaths. But one event haunted him incessantly, and no matter how hard he tried, he couldn't remove it from his mind.

Jeff described a mission in which he had been assigned to destroy a munitions dump that the Vietcong had stored in an orphanage. The plan was for soldiers on the ground to evacuate the orphanage's children prior to his attack. As Jeff approached his target, he received confirmation of the children's evacuation, so he bombed the building containing the stored munitions.

But when he returned to his base, he discovered that he had received false information: The orphanage had not been evacuated, and many children had died. Devastated, Jeff blamed himself. He thought of himself as a baby killer, a child murderer, an evil person. *I shouldn't have bombed it. I should have known,* he kept thinking. Consumed with guilt, he hated himself.

Was his guilt appropriate? Jeff wasn't accurate or honest with himself. He treated himself as if he knew the children had not been evacuated from the building, judging himself on the outcome of his actions rather than on his motives, choices, and intent. In other words, he responded as though he had intended to kill the children, as if he should have known the report he had received was false. While the outcome was tragic, his decision and actions at the time had been appropriate. His guilt was misplaced.

Consider yourself a firefighter in charge of explosive fire suppression. (Large fires are sometimes extinguished by detonating an explosion that burns up all available oxygen and therefore extinguishes the fire.) A building is on fire, and those battling it determine that the only way to extinguish the flames is through an explosion.

You are responsible for setting the charges while other firefighters clear the building. After setting the charges, you receive the "all clear" to detonate the charges, so you do. But afterward it is discovered that several children had not been evacuated and had perished from the explosion. Would you feel guilty? Had you done anything wrong? Unwanted outcomes sometimes occur in this life, even when we do our best. Unfortunately, we all too often judge ourselves according to the outcome rather than the intent.

Guilt and Grief Are Not the Same

John was 43 years of age, with brown hair and a medium build. His furrowed brow and the dark circles under his eyes were consequences of his having suffered from depression for 20 years—since the death of his 3-year-old son. During our conversations he recounted how two decades earlier his son had become ill with a high fever and irritability, so he took him to his pediatrician. The physician told John that it was an ear infection, gave the child antibiotics, and sent them home.

After they returned home, his son's condition worsened, the fever rose, and he began to vomit. John took the child to a nearby emergency room, where the staff told the father again that his son had an ear infection, offered some reassurance, and sent them home.

Later that evening his son's condition continued to worsen. His skin burned, and he became less responsive, so John again rushed him to the emergency room. This time the doctors discovered that the boy had meningitis. But because his condition was so advanced, he died later that night.

Absolutely devastated, John blamed himself and was burdened with chronic, unremitting guilt. He ridiculed himself constantly. "I should have known. I knew something was wrong. I shouldn't have listened to the doctors. I should have done something. It's my fault. My son would be alive if I weren't so stupid."

John judged himself as having failed his child, but what more could the father have done? Although he had no medical training, he had taken his child three times in one day to physicians who missed the diagnosis. Was he to blame for their failure? He had fallen into the trap of judging himself based on the outcome rather than on his actions and intent.

Now John needed to realize the differences that distinguish guilt from sadness, grief, and heartache. While sadness, grief, and heartache were all healthy and appropriate emotions with which he needed to grapple, guilt was not. Because the guilt was inappropriate, it actually interfered with his grief resolution. It was only when he realized that he had done nothing wrong—that if he were again in the same circumstances, with the same information, he would have made the same decision—that he was able to let go of the guilt and begin resolving the grief.

Darla's Illegitimate Guilt

At age 44 Darla had a long history of depression and anxiety, suffering from posttraumatic stress disorder that had resulted from years of severe spousal abuse. She described horrible assaults against her and multiple occasions her husband had become drunk, pointed a gun at her head, and threatened to kill her. While she had many legitimate reasons for her anxiety and depression, she also suffered from unremitting inappropriate guilt.

Darla struggled to recount the agonizing experiences she had endured. As she described the horrible abuse, she frequently shook her head back and forth in order to pull herself out of a flashback experience.

Several years earlier she had discovered that her husband was molesting his daughter (her stepdaughter). But when she notified his family, instead of helping they told her to keep quiet or they would kill her.

93

Although terrified, she refused to let her stepdaughter remain in such abuse, so she reported her husband to the Department of Family and Children's Services (DFACS). Following an investigation of the charges, the authorities arrested her husband and prosecuted him for his crimes. But Darla blamed herself. *I should have known that my stepdaughter was being molested. How could I not have known?* she thought.

For years Darla experienced chronic guilt for not having prevented events that she had no knowledge were occurring. Not until she used her reason to evaluate the facts and apply the truth did she begin to heal. She recognized that she was not responsible for her husband's actions or for information that she did not possess.

Once Darla learned to judge herself based on her own actions, her own decisions, she was then able to resolve her inappropriate guilt and move forward in the healing process.

Parents Don't Control Outcomes

More parents than I can count have children who make decisions that disappoint or even shame their parents. My patients may have children who have chosen to "shack up," are in jail, are on drugs, or are behaving irresponsibly. Although each story is unique, most of the parents share one common problem—they blame themselves and punish themselves, thinking: *If only I had done something different, my child would not have turned out this way.*

Such individuals experience inappropriate guilt because they have accepted a lie. They have believed that they, as parents, are responsible for the outcome of their children's lives and in the process have failed to recognize that they are accountable only for their own conduct in raising their children. Because all have free wills, the children ultimately choose their own course, regardless of the parenting.

Some of my patients have forgotten that while parenting influences, it does not ensure the outcome. Even when parenting is absolutely perfect—as in the case of God's parenting Lucifer and Adam—children can still choose to go astray.

Illegitimate Guilt—Type III

Sarah was distraught from years of unremitting guilt. For seven years the memories of an adulterous relationship had tormented her. Although she knew the affair was wrong, she couldn't seem to resist her attraction to the other man. But immediately after breaking her marital vows, she found herself overcome with guilt and plagued with self-loathing. As a result she confessed her sin to God and to her husband. She repented and her husband forgave her, and she determined never to stray again. Yet during the seven years since the affair she had experienced constant guilt and recurring memories of the incident. Despite repeated hours on her knees confessing to God and begging His forgiveness, her guilt never seemed to go away, and she didn't know why. Soon she wondered whether she was beyond salvation.

If repentance and restoration resolve appropriate guilt, and Sarah had repented and reconciled with her husband, then why didn't the guilt go away? Because even though she felt sorrow for her affair, the way her mind operated had not changed. The mental process that had led to the affair still lingered in her ways of thinking.

In chapters 2 and 3 we explored the organizational model of the mind. We discovered that reason and conscience constitute our judgment and are to direct the will in making healthy choices. Also we learned that our feelings can lead us astray or tempt us. Now consider the mental process of those choosing to commit adultery. Do they use their reason and conscience, weigh the evidence, pray for wisdom and guidance, and with a clear conscience make an enlightened decision to commit adultery? Or do they experience strong feelings of arousal and ignore their reason and conscience?

Now what happens when the same process occurs on a different issue? One day at the office a coworker asked Sarah to borrow her car. Immediately Sarah reasoned through the facts that her insurance permitted no other drivers and that the person making the request had been in several car accidents recently, and concluded, in her judgment, no! But then feelings of fear and insecurity overwhelmed her. *I don't want her to be angry. I want her to like me. I don't want her to start rumors about me. And I hate confrontation.* So based on all her feelings she ignored her own judgment and let the coworker borrow the car.

Here we find her mind operating in the exact same way it did when she committed adultery. She feels guilt for not choosing to do what her judgment decided was best. Failing to understand how God designed her mind to work and with the issue of lending her car not being a moral issue, Sarah was impaired in her ability to identify the source of her guilt. Rather than experience guilt for letting a coworker drive her car, her mind regurgitates the most egregious example of her letting feelings trump judgment, and she again experiences guilt for the extramarital affair. Thus for the past seven years each time she allowed feelings to overrule judgment, she again went through guilt for the affair, which caused her to repent of it once more. Because she has never dealt with the way her mind operates, she never experiences peace or a real sense of forgiveness. It is only by putting our minds back in balance that they can heal.

Truth Removes Inappropriate Guilt

It is the exercise of reason evaluating the facts and circumstances and then understanding and applying the truth that will remove inappropriate guilt from the mind and allow healing to take place.

God has designed our universe in a very orderly fashion. When we operate in harmony with His principles and methods, we experience health of mind and peace of heart. As our minds function in the hierarchical order He intended, our self-esteem, self-worth, and self-confidence automatically rise. Conversely, whenever we allow our minds to operate without reason and conscience directing our actions, then our self-esteem, self-worth, and self-confidence fall.

The cornerstone principles of God's government are love, truth, and freedom. The process of applying truth to the mind and practicing methods that are in harmony with His methods is known as spiritual warfare. We will explore it in the next chapter.

CHAPTER 11

Spiritual Warfare

Mary's life was out of control when she first came to my office. She had been sexually molested as a child, raped as a teenager, and raped again in her 20s. Now, at age 35, she had a teenage son from a failed marriage and two children under 5 from her current marriage.

During the eight years before she came to me, Mary had consulted five other psychiatrists for treatment. During that time she had also visited 12 therapists. The psychiatrists had offered a wide variety of diagnoses for her problems: schizophrenia, bipolar (manic-depressive) disorder, multiple personality disorder, histrionic personality disorder, borderline personality disorder, posttraumatic stress disorder, benzodiazepine dependence, and unipolar depression.

She complained of hearing voices that sometimes told her to kill herself. In addition, she suffered from chronic headaches and multiple medical problems, resulting in her having undergone more than 20 surgical procedures during the previous eight years.

For the past five years much of her life had come to a complete standstill. Unable to cook, clean, take the kids to school, or help with any household chores, she had not functioned as a wife and mother. Her husband was responsible for her care.

Additionally, Mary arrived at the emergency room once or twice each week to get Demerol injections for the headaches that never seemed to go away. She had been treated with multiple medications—including Haldol, Thorazine, Valium, Elavil, Sinequan, Prozac, Restoril, Vistaril, Xanax, and others she could not remember—all without any improvement. When she first came to me, she was on high doses of Valium and Thorazine, as well as painkillers for the headaches.

Mary had chronically low self-esteem and feelings of worthlessness—all reinforced by lifelong abuse and mistreatment. She had never developed the ability to use her reason and conscience to direct her will to examine and choose the truth to battle her tumultuous moods, feelings, and thoughts.

Struggling with persistent guilt, she criticized herself unreasonably. Whenever she encountered difficulty in a relationship, Mary always blamed herself and felt guilty, regardless of what actually had occurred. Although she was a Christian, nobody had ever taught her how to engage in spiritual warfare.

We Do Not Wage War as the World Does

Spiritual warfare is the engagement of the spiritual nature (reason, conscience, worship) to battle unhealthy feelings, lies, misrepresentations, passions, and lusts that try to take control of the will and dethrone the reason. It is the process of using God's methods to overcome the influence of our genetic weakness, heal our emotional wounds, and restore balance to our damaged minds.

"For though we live in the world, we do not wage war as the world does. The weapons we fight with are not the weapons of the world. On the contrary, they have divine power to demolish strongholds. We demolish *arguments* and every *pretension* that sets itself up against the *knowledge* of God, and we take captive every *thought* to make it obedient to Christ" (2 Cor. 10:3-5).

If you're fighting a war over arguments, pretensions, knowledge, and thoughts, where is that war being waged? In the mind! Spiritual warfare rages in the mind. The weapon we utilize is the "Sword of the Spirit," the Word of God, also known as the truth. Because it always leads to God, such truth has divine power. Through its divine power, truth destroys lies, misrepresentations, and distortions. It also restores order and brings healing. As Christ said: "The truth will set you free" (John 8:32).

God Is Working to Heal Everyone

It is important to recognize that truth heals, regardless of whether or not one believes in God. The Holy Spirit strives for healing even in those who have not yet formed a belief in divinity. The Holy Spirit moves to bring God's methods and principles to their understanding. If those who do not believe in Him follow the truth they do comprehend, then healing results, and they become healthier and healthier in proportion to what they understand and practice. Eventually the truth will lead them to God Himself for complete healing and restoration.

Paul describes this in Romans 2:13-15: "For it is not those who hear the law who are righteous in God's sight, but it is those who obey the law who will be declared righteous. (Indeed, when Gentiles, who do not have the law, do by nature things required by the law, they are a law for themselves, even though they do not have the law, since they show that the requirements of the law are written on their hearts, their consciences also bearing witness, and their thoughts now accusing, now even defending them.)"

Paul here declares that God is working to heal everyone's mind. Those who haven't heard the truth (as revealed in Scripture), but understand the principles of love and liberty (as demonstrated in nature) and incorporate them into their lives, are cooperating with God for the healing of their minds. The Lord is restoring His image within them and considers them His children.

Truth Sets Us Free

Sergeant Jones, whom we read about in chapter 1, had believed a lie— that God had let him down. The lie resulted in his inability to resolve his war experiences. Recognizing the truth—that God had actually miraculously intervened in his life—destroyed the stronghold of misunderstanding, fear, doubt, guilt, anger, and resentment that had established itself within him. It set Sergeant Jones free.

Consider the example of a man who has stolen from his brother. Guilt-ridden, restless, and uneasy, he no longer has peace. What is it that will set him free from guilt and restore peace, regardless of whether he believes in God or not? It is repentance and restoration. He is experiencing legitimate guilt, and only the truth accepted and applied will overcome it and restore health.

By going to his brother, acknowledging what he has done, restoring what he has taken, and asking forgiveness, he will find peace for his mind. Even if his brother refuses to forgive him, he will have peace with himself because he has a changed heart, a healed mind. The change of heart occurred when he made a willful choice to do what reason and conscience determined was best. He will not have restored unity with his brother until his brother forgives him, but his own self-torment will cease.

The Mind Is Like a Garden

Imagine that you have a garden, one that you have faithfully tended and that now produces a bountiful harvest. What will happen to your garden if you stop cultivating it? Will it continue to bear good fruit, or will the weeds eventually destroy it?

In a similar way, our minds naturally bring up weeds—selfish thoughts, ideas, and conceptions. It is Christ who works through the Holy Spirit to plant the seeds of truth in our minds. He then nurtures and protects the seeds, enabling them to grow into the fruits of a Christlike character. By utilizing the Sword of the Spirit (which is the Word of God, the truth) we weed our minds, uprooting the lies and false theories that keep us captive, and thus allow us instead to maintain a healthy and productive mental garden.

One of the best descriptions of this process appears in Ellen G. White's *The Desire of Ages.*

"The Comforter is called 'the Spirit of truth.' His work is to define and maintain the truth. He first dwells in the heart as the Spirit of truth, and thus He becomes the Comforter. There is comfort and peace in the truth, but no real peace or comfort can be found in falsehood. It is through false theories and traditions that Satan gains his power over the mind. By directing men to false standards, he misshapes the character. Through the Scriptures the Holy Spirit speaks to the mind, and impresses truth upon the heart. Thus He exposes error, and expels it from the soul. It is by the Spirit of truth, working through the Word of God, that Christ subdues His chosen people to Himself."*

The Problem With Sin

One of the misconceptions (weeds) that impair a greater harvest of spiritual fruit is the misconception about sin. Many people view it as breaking one of God's rules, and the trouble with disobeying one of His rules is that it requires Him to impose a penalty, the minimum being death. But this is a fundamental misunderstanding about sin, which leads to serious misconceptions about God—distortions that get incorporated into worship and consequently impair the healing of the mind.

The real problem with sin is that sin itself damages and destroys. It destroys the sinner and damages others. Because sin mars the image of God within, persistence in sin brings its own punishment—death. Persons who cling to sinful living lower themselves from beings created with dignity, nobility, and intelligence to nothing more than mere animals, mindless creatures of instinct. Reason and conscience eventually disappear, and the animal passions take full control.

Why God Hates Sin

Many people assume that God hates sin because it involves breaking

His rules, which shows disrespect toward Him. But imagine you're the mayor of your hometown who has enacted a law prohibiting cruelty to animals. As you walk out of your home, someone takes your pet kitten, swings it by the tail, and smashes its head on the concrete. What outrages you? What angers you? Do you scream, "You just broke my law! How dare you break my law!" Is it the violation of the law that outrages you? Or is it the fact your beautiful pet has been killed? That is why God hates sin: because it destroys His creation, not because it breaks His rules.

In fact, the rules were set up to help us see the destructiveness of our behavior. Remember when God proclaimed the Ten Commandments? The children of Israel had just emerged from 400 years of slavery. Life in such an environment was cheap. The most minor violations could lead to a slave's death. Living in such a world, the Hebrews had lost sight of the high calling that God had created humanity to fulfill, and they had sunk into an ignorant darkness.

Consider how abysmal their condition must have been if God found it necessary to tell them that if you love your neighbors, you won't kill them. Nor will you steal from them, ruin their reputations by misrepresenting them, or commit adultery with their spouses. The Hebrew slaves didn't have even these basic precepts in their lives.

Imagine sending your child off to school this morning, kissing him goodbye, and saying, "Have fun at school today, and be sure not to murder anyone at recess." How absolutely absurd. It would never enter your mind. But if you actually needed to say this to your child, how debased would your child be?

An MRI for the Soul

The written law (Ten Commandments) is like an MRI (an imaging diagnostic test) of the soul: It reveals the defects. If an MRI scan revealed a tumor in your lung, what would you do? Go to your physician. And after you had visited the physician and been healed, would you worry about having been examined by the MRI? Would you feel any need to destroy the MRI? Of course not. In fact, you might want to repeat the MRI procedure to confirm that the tumor was gone.

That is how God's written law works. It reveals the defects in our mind. When we recognize those defects, we go to the heavenly Physician for healing. After He has healed us, the written law doesn't need to be destroyed. In fact, when it examines us, it finds no defects because we are in harmony with it. And having been healed, we no longer need the written law. It is the essence of what Paul tells Timothy: "We know that the law is good if one uses it properly. We also know that law is made not for the righteous but for lawbreakers and rebels, the ungodly and sinful, the unholy and irreligious; for those who kill their fathers or mothers, for murderers, for adulterers and perverts, for slave traders and liars and perjurers—and for whatever else is contrary to the sound doctrine that conforms to the glorious gospel of the blessed God, which he entrusted to me" (1 Tim. 1:8-11).

Using our metaphor of an MRI, we might paraphrase the passage like this: "We know that the MRI is good if one uses it properly. We also know that the MRI is made not for healthy people but for those who are sick and diseased, the suffering, the ill, and all those who are dying, and all activities that are contrary to the principles of healthy living that conform to the model of health that the blessed God has entrusted to me."

In fact, the ten-commandment portion of the law is a special distillation of the great cosmic law of love and liberty written especially for those of us here on this planet. Did the angels in heaven require a law to honor their mother and father? Or to instruct them not to commit adultery? No, but they did need to operate by the law of love and liberty as discussed earlier in this book. The Ten Commandments are a further extrapolation of this law, as Christ Himself emphasized: "'Love the Lord your God with all your heart and with all your soul and with all your mind.' This is the first and greatest commandment. And the second is like it: 'Love your neighbor as yourself.' All the Law and the Prophets hang on these two commandments" (Matt. 22:37-40).

Sin—Not God—Destroys

Many of my patients fail to understand the nature of sin and its effects. Because many think that God is the one that destroys, they have chronic feelings of insecurity and fear. But consider the following:

If you never brushed your teeth, would it surprise you if you developed cavities? Would God send an angel down from heaven to give you cavities? What if you prayed every day for healthy teeth, but didn't brush them? What would you expect to happen? Cavities!

Suppose you jumped off the Empire State Building. Would it surprise you if you went splat when you hit the pavement? Would God send an angel to break your legs when you crashed into it? What if you prayed on the way down for good health and a long life? What would you expect to happen? Splat!

Imagine if you cheated on your spouse. Would you not expect to experience lowered self-esteem, guilt, anxiety, and shame? Would God send an angel down from heaven to devastate your self-esteem and ruin your marriage?

Sin destroys because it involves living outside of the universal principles on which God has based life and health. Those principles are both natural and moral. Furthermore, sin exists outside of the divine law of love and liberty. In fact, sin is lawlessness.

God's law of love and liberty is not merely a set of arbitrary rules created by a powerful deity. Quite the contrary, His law of love and liberty emanates from His character. In fact, the principles that govern our existence and the running of the universe are an outworking of this law.

Earlier we discussed in some detail the law of liberty and saw how violations of it always bring destruction in their wake. Likewise with violations of the law of love: destruction always follows. That is the problem with sin: it destroys. But God is not the cause of such destruction. *He heals!*

Many of my patients can see very easily how violations of the law of gravity will injure, but they have a more difficult time seeing how breaking God's moral law will damage human beings.

Imagine that you molested a child today and no one ever found out. The incident always remained a secret. How well would you sleep tonight? And if you could sleep after doing such a thing, how damaged a person must you already be?

Engaging in immoral behavior destroys the image of God within. It strengthens the base passions and weakens reason and conscience. Sin persisted in, over time, will ultimately eradicate the ability to comprehend or respond to truth. When this occurs, nothing more can be done. Once reason and conscience have been totally destroyed by persistent rebellious living, the human being—created with nobility, dignity, and intelligence—sinks downward to join the brute beasts, creatures of instinct driven only by passion and lust.

Sin Is Like Cancer

Sin is like cancer. It leads to death for the same reason that cancer does—it actually destroys the tissues and organs that sustain life. When someone dies from cancer, death is not an externally imposed penalty but the inevitable result of unimpeded cancer. Unless someone *intercedes,* cancer will kill. That is what *intercession* is about—God steps in to stop the natural progression/consequences of sin in our lives. He works to heal us!

As sin spreads through a person, it damages and eventually destroys the mental faculties that recognize and respond to truth. And if persisted in, sin will degrade the entire being and eventually result in death.

Now, if a person with cancer undergoes treatment and is cured, what happened to the cancer? The defective cells were either removed or restored to normal. In order for the body to live, the cancer must remit. When cancer is in remission, the defective cancerous cells are gone and the previously diseased tissues have returned to their original condition.

Sin is a state of mind characterized by selfishness and the practicing of methods in opposition to the principles upon which God has based life and health. Just as with cancer, if something is not done to change this selfish state of mind the inevitable result is death. The Bible states that "without shedding of blood there is no remission" of sin (Heb. 9:22, KJV). In other words, without the shedding of blood we could not be restored to our original condition. The shedding of Christ's blood is meant to transform the human heart and mind—to heal us and remove selfishness completely from our minds.

When we understand the truth about God and His methods and surrender to Him, a new motive—set of principles/methods—becomes the governing power in the human mind, removing "sin" (the rebellious selfish method).

The Obedience of an Understanding Friend

Health comes from conformity to God's law, from living in harmony with the great principles of love and liberty. It does not result from blind conformity to a set of rules or because someone in authority or with power told you so; it comes about because it makes sense.

In fact, obedience that springs only from a sullen submission is not real obedience—it is actually violating the law of liberty and always leads to rebellion. True obedience must involve understanding and agreement. The highest level of obedience has its origin in understanding friendship.

One of my friends told me that when he was a child, his mother had a rule that he was not to smoke. If he did smoke, he would be punished accordingly. As you might expect, my friend avoided smoking during his childhood. Desiring to be an obedient little boy, he obeyed the rule. And he certainly didn't want to get punished.

As a teenager, though, he found himself in the company of several friends who passed around a cigarette. After some prompting, my friend took a couple of puffs. Later, when he went home, his mother smelled the cigarette smoke, took him aside, and said, "Son, if you ever begin smoking, you'll break my heart." That comment provided the motivation for him, as an adolescent, not to smoke again, because he loved her very much.

But even now as an adult, he continues to avoid smoking. Why? Do you think he phones his mother and tells her, "I really wanted to smoke today, but I chose not to, because I knew if I did, you would come over and punish me"? Or does he call her and announce, "I really wanted to smoke today, but I didn't because I love you and don't want to hurt you"? If he did, do you think his mother would reply, "Well done; I'm proud of you, son"? Or would she be more likely to say, "Son, when will you ever grow up?"

Today he doesn't smoke—*not* because of mother's rule, not because of his mother's love for him or his love for her, but *because he is a nonsmoker.* Having used his reason and conscience to evaluate the logic behind his mother's rule, he has come to understand why she would have been hurt. He now recognizes that smoking is destructive. And he has used his will to choose not to smoke, because he agrees with his mother.

Through such insights and understanding, his love and appreciation for his mother and her rules greatly increase. His love for his mother grows because he sees the great love his mother had for him to protect him from himself when he was too childlike to know better. Now he no longer needs the rules of childhood—not because they are wrong or invalidated, but because they are written in his heart.

Growing Up

We are called to become mature Christians, to develop the ability to discern the right from the wrong. But all too often we remain as little babes concerned about breaking the rules or worried about hurting our Father. When will we actually grow up and understand our Father? When will we enter into unity, harmony, and friendship with Him? And when will we cooperate with Him for the restoration of His image within, the writing of His law and methods on our hearts and minds?

Free From All Those Rules

Imagine again that your mother raised you with a rule that you must brush your teeth. Now that you are grown and on your own, you proclaim, "I'm free from Mother's rule. I'm never going to brush my teeth again." And you don't. What happens? Dirty teeth, bad breath, and eventually cavities.

While this is going on, does your mother stop loving you? Or does her heart ache, knowing that you will soon be in pain? If you persist in going against what she taught you about brushing your teeth, does she come over while you're sleeping and drill holes in your teeth? No, the teeth rot on their own.

When the pain develops, is it an imposed penalty or a consequence? And what will the pain lead you to do? Hopefully, visit the dentist.

Does the dentist inflict more pain to punish you for not brushing your teeth, or does he or she do everything possible to minimize it while setting about to heal the self-inflicted damage? But if you should choose not to visit the dentist, and decide instead to endure the pain, perhaps using alcohol to deaden the toothache, eventually the teeth will be so damaged that nothing will remain for the dentist to fix.

The Unpardonable Sin

When we violate God's law, He never stops loving us. His heart breaks as He watches us hurt ourselves, knowing that we will soon be in pain. But He allows the pain to come so that hopefully it might bring us to our senses and we will seek Him for healing. And if we do go to Him, He will never harm us, but does all in His power to minimize the pain as He begins healing our minds.

Often, though, the damage is so extensive that even healing itself is accompanied by pain. But if we choose to avoid going to God, and instead numb our pain with alcohol, drugs, sex, work, or TV, eventually the damage will become so extensive that nothing remains to heal. Reason and conscience have been totally destroyed. We have lost the ability to respond.

When this happens, what more can God do? Here we encounter what the Bible calls the "unpardonable sin"—*unpardonable* not because God is unwilling to forgive, but because sinners have so injured themselves that they have lost the faculties necessary to recognize and to respond to the pardoning grace He so freely offers.

If we violate God's methods long enough, we become so damaged that we reject any further effort by Him in our behalf. If we destroy our own individuality, God cannot restore it without violating the law of liberty.

Assume that someone rejects all entreaties that God sends, that they neglect all efforts of mercy and grace, and that the image of God within has been erased. If God were to restore them to their status before they destroyed themselves, then they would simply repeat the destruction, because their character has not changed.

If, on the other hand, God were to effect transformations of character so that they would not harm themselves, then He would have made new beings, and the former individuals would no longer exist. And as we have seen, to change an individual's character without the individual's consent destroys love, something that God will never do.

There's a Difference Between Rules and Law

We must understand the difference between God's rules and God's law. His law is the universal principles that govern life—for example, the law of gravity, the law of love, and the law of liberty. God's rules are the tools He uses, while we are children, to protect us from the damage that results from violating His law. Until we grow up to understand and incorporate His law into our own hearts and minds, we need the rules. But after we grow up, the rules are no longer necessary.

Imagine that one of your rules for your 5-year-old was that she had to brush her teeth before bedtime each night. Suppose that I approached your child and told her, "You don't have to brush your teeth because Mommy said so. Rather, you have to brush your teeth because of the second law of thermodynamics, which states that things tend toward disorder. So if you don't brush your teeth, they will decay."

Your child might look at me with a puzzled expression and say, "You're not supporting Mommy. You're against Mommy's rules. You want to get me in trouble with Mommy."

But if your 5-year-old does disobey and chooses not to brush her teeth, what do you think would be her primary concern: that her teeth might decay, or that her mommy would be angry and punish her? And after she disobeyed, what would be her most likely response—simply to brush her teeth, or to pick some flowers or draw a picture to appease Mommy?

Unfortunately, the church is filled with babes in Christ who never grow up to understand the law behind the rules. When they first become acquainted with the reasons for the rules, they often say, "You're not supporting God. You're against His law. You have no standards and want to get us in trouble with Him."

And if such Christians do violate God's law and commit an act of sin, they are more concerned about whether He is angry than with the fact their sin is destroying their lives. As a result, they develop an entire theological system based on appeasing God's anger and wrath rather than co-operating with Him for the restoration of His image within. Failing to see that sin is actually destroying them, and instead misjudging God as angry and vengeful, they spend their time developing theories designed to appease Him by making a payment, even stating that He Himself supplied the perfect payment. The main focus is not on healing the damage of sin, but instead on avoiding the punishment of an angry and offended God.

This situation is similar to your child growing up to believe that if she doesn't brush her teeth, you will become angry and seek to make her pay for her disobedience. How relieved would you be if your child finally understood that you were not angry with her? How thrilled would you be if she realized that you simply wanted her to be healthy, that you had designed the rules as tools to help her while she still lacked the maturity to understand? How sad would you be if your child never understood and remained afraid that you were going to punish her?

Mary

As Mary (the young woman described in the beginning of this chapter) and I worked together, she came to recognize that she had longstanding unresolved anger and resentment from the mistreatment that had occurred in various relationships throughout her life. She had interpreted the abuse by others as evidence that there was something wrong with her. It led to a significantly distorted self-image accompanied by chronic feelings of inadequacy and insecurity. Every relationship in her life was characterized by dependency issues that further confused and damaged her ability to recover.

We began by establishing a therapeutic trust. Then in the context of this relationship we explored many painful experiences and reexamined them in light of truth and evidence, reasoning from cause to effect. Mary learned to tolerate unpleasant feelings and chose to apply the things that she concluded were healthy despite how she felt about them.

Her therapy lasted longer than with most of my patients, but approximately 18 months later she was a new person. She had learned how to exercise her reason and conscience to explore facts and circumstances and to draw reasonable conclusions. And she had discovered how to exercise her will to implement those conclusions in the face of uncomfortable feelings. This resulted in an ever-increasing sense of self-confidence and self-esteem.

When I last heard from Mary, she had not been on any medications for more than two years and had not visited the ER for injections of pain medicine. Her headaches had all but subsided, occurring only rarely and relieved with Tylenol. She had heard no voices in more than two years, and she was active in all aspects of her life.

Besides completely running the household, she attended an aerobics class three times per week. She was teaching a women's class at her church each week, and she even gave the sermon one week. The coordinator of the church's building fund, she had organized multiple fund drives, such as car washes and bake sales.

At the time we terminated therapy her husband stated that he now had the woman he had fallen in love with when they had first met. Most important, they both praised God and stated that they believed it was the inclusion of the spiritual aspect of treatment into her care that made the difference.

My diagnosis of Mary was posttraumatic stress disorder (PTSD). The voices she reported were flashback experiences related to her trauma. Those symptoms had also ceased by the end of her treatment.

After she began to exercise her reason and tolerate negative feelings, one of the key issues for Mary in resolving her trauma involved forgiving those who had done her wrong. Her long-held feelings of resentment and bitterness had been a poison welling up inside of her and ruining her life.

She had clung to many myths about forgiveness that impaired her ability to forgive. As we explored those myths and the real meaning of forgiveness, Mary was finally able to find healing and peace for her heart. Let's explore some of the myths about forgiveness in the next chapter.

---

* Ellen G. White, *The Desire of Ages* (Mountain View, Calif.: Pacific Press Pub. Assn., 1898), p. 671.

CHAPTER 12

Forgiveness

"The stupid neither forgive nor forget; the naïve forgive and forget; the wise forgive but do not forget."—Thomas Szasz.

W hy? Why does this keep happening to me?" Kate mumbled between sobs as she told me the painful story of her husband's most recent betrayal. In her early 40s, she was the daughter of a Baptist minister, raised in a conservative Southern home. She had married her high school sweetheart shortly after graduation, and they had quickly had two beautiful children.

Unfortunately, soon after the birth of their second child Kate discovered that her husband was having an affair. She painfully asked him to leave the home. But he quickly ran to her pastor to confess his mistake and, in tears, explained that he had asked Jesus to forgive him, but that his wife had thrown him out.

Accepting the husband's claim as sincere, the pastor visited Kate and reminded her that the Lord Jesus had also forgiven her. Then he asked her to forgive her husband and permit him to return to his family. She did so.

As time passed, however, her husband continued to stray from his marriage vows, and Kate was now in my office crying over her husband's sixth affair. She reported that after each of the first five affairs the same pattern ensued. First she would throw him out; then he would go crying to her pastor, telling how he had asked Jesus to forgive him. And each time the pastor urged that she forgive her husband and take him back.

This time, however, she was in my office. Kate recognized the importance of forgiving her husband. In forgiving him, she would relieve herself of bitterness, resentment, and pain, thus allowing herself to heal. But more important, she also learned that the act of forgiving her husband *did not change him*—that her forgiveness did not make him trustworthy. And until he became trustworthy, she would be foolish to allow him back into the home. Therefore, Kate forgave her husband, but she didn't let him return.

Many of my patients arrive with long-term mood disturbances. When we begin to explore the underlying factors, I frequently discover long-standing resentment and inability to forgive.

They are unable to forgive because they have encountered a wide variety of myths related to it. The law of worship has significant ramifications for this issue. Remember that the law of worship states that we become like the object we worship or admire. People tend to forgive others in the way they believe that God does. Not surprisingly then, most of the myths about forgiveness involve misconceptions about how God forgives.

Myth 1: Forgiveness Comes After the Offending Individuals Say They Are Sorry

All too often I have heard people declare, "I'll be glad to forgive when he says he's sorry." The problem with believing this myth is that it fails to realize that forgiveness heals the offended party, not the offender. Offenders experience healing when they repent. When both forgiveness and repentance occur, then so does reconciliation.

In Christian terms, reconciliation—rather than forgiveness—is necessary for salvation, a point sorely misunderstood by many well-meaning Christians who believe that forgiveness is all that is required.

Let's say a longtime friend comes to my office and for some reason suddenly hits me, curses me, and then runs out of my office. Of course, I have no idea why he did this, but I have to decide how I am going to respond. I could choose to become angry and seek revenge, to call the police, or to get a stick and chase him down. Right there in my office I have to decide how I will react.

Perhaps I choose to forgive him. Does my forgiveness restore our relationship? No, but because I have forgiven him, I go after him, not to punish, but to find out why he hit me and seek to restore our friendship. But my friend sees me approaching him, misinterprets my intentions, and assumes that I am angry, so he flees as fast as he can.

That is our state with God. We chose to rebel against Him, but He never—not for one instant—became angry. Instead, He forgave immediately. But His forgiveness didn't restore our relationship with Him, because we misjudged Him and fled from Him. And we've been running ever since.

What if my friend decided to repent and sought to make amends for his mistreatment of me, but I refused to forgive? Will our relationship resume? No, it takes both forgiveness and repentance for reconciliation to occur.

It is also true in our relationship with God. Unfortunately, many people regard Him as unforgiving or as demanding some payment or sacrifice in order to forgive. But that is simply not true. In fact, it is God's forgiving attitude, which comes first, that leads us to repentance. The apostle Paul declares that "God's kindness leads you toward repentance" (Rom. 2:4).

The Lord has taken the initiative to come after us to bring us back into friendship with Him, but all too often we have misinterpreted His actions, much like a child misunderstands when a parent gives them vaccines. Therefore, God sent His Son to be one with us, to demonstrate the kind of person the Father is, so that by revealing His character He will lead us to repentance and subsequent reconciliation.

Unfortunately, many well-meaning people are confused about this and believe that God doesn't forgive until we plead for His forgiveness. Such people also deal with their friends in a similar manner, refusing to forgive until someone asks. And this common misunderstanding about God constitutes myth 2 about forgiveness.

Myth 2: God's Forgiveness Equals Salvation

But that simply is not true. Salvation requires not only forgiveness from God but also repentance on the part of the sinner. When Christ hung on the cross, what did He say to His Father about those who put Him there? "Father, forgive them, for they do not know what they are doing" (Luke 23:34). Did His persecutors ask for forgiveness? No! Nevertheless, God the Son forgave them. Although they did not request it, they were forgiven by the One who has the power in heaven and earth to do so.

While they were forgiven, were they saved? Did Christ's act of forgiveness change His persecutors' hearts? Were they now friends of God? Or were they still His enemies, still mocking Him, still crucifying Him? They remained His enemies because they didn't open their hearts to receive the forgiveness that He so freely offered. Had they opened their hearts to God's forgiveness, it would have led them to repent (have a change of heart), and reconciliation would have occurred. It's unfortunate that their hearts were so hard that they didn't respond.

John was a member of a conservative Christian denomination who believed that in order to be saved he must repent of each specific and individual act of sin. His belief caused him great insecurity in his Christian walk. He constantly worried that he might forget to confess something that would prevent his salvation.

Finally he became so troubled that he suffered a heart attack and was rushed to a hospital emergency room, where his heart stopped four times. Each time the medical staff defibrillated his heart, and each time it started again. Later he recounted that between each defibrillation he woke up thinking, *I hope there isn't some sin I forgot to confess that will keep me out of the kingdom.* John believed that God doesn't forgive until we ask.

Consider a first-grade boy who sees one of his classmates with a pen that lights up when squeezed. Coveting the pen, he steals it. As he grows up, he continues to steal things along the way until one day, as an adult, the authorities arrest and punish him.

After being caught, he repents and experiences a true change of heart. From that point onward he is honest in all his dealings. He goes out of his way to avoid even a hint of dishonesty. If he encountered a gray area on his taxes, he always chose to pay extra rather than do anything that might get construed as cheating. Accepting Christ as his Savior, he lived in harmony with God the rest of his life. But he never remembered about the pen in first grade. Do you think that when he comes up in the judgment God would meet him with the following verdict?

"You have been a true and trusted friend, like David of old, a man after my own heart. You have been honest and faithful and have been healed in the inner man. Your heart is right, and you love and practice methods in harmony with Mine, but you never asked to be forgiven for stealing the pen in first grade. I'm sorry, but you can't enter heaven."

We can't imagine God being so arbitrary. The issue isn't whether we remember every mistake we ever made. Instead, the issue concerns the condition of our heart and mind. Have we been healed? Has God restored His image within us?

Myth 3: Forgiving Someone Means That What That Person Did Was OK

Does forgiving others mean approval of what they did? Obviously not. But many people do believe that if others are forgiven, then what they did has been neutralized or canceled, and it is therefore OK.

Such a misunderstanding results from the basic misunderstanding about sin we have already discussed. If sin is primarily a legal problem, and forgiveness is a judicial act by a powerful potentate, then forgiveness erases the record. And *poof!* No punishment—the person's off the hook.

But as we have already discovered, sin damages the sinner, and even if the person is forgiven, the effect has already occurred. The injury to our minds can be healed only by the work of the Holy Spirit through repentance and application of the truth. Those forgiven by God but who never repent do not allow God to heal their damaged minds and thus remain lost. The various groups who crucified Christ would fall into this category.

But even for those who do repent, while they experience healing of their heart and mind, they don't necessarily escape the consequences of sin. For instance, King David committed adultery with a friend's wife. When she became pregnant, David murdered Uriah, the husband, to cover up the sin. After doing all of this, David was forgiven and repented. He experienced real heart change and was reconciled to God, but Uriah was dead, and David's crime against him remained. David's sin led to a rebellion within the kingdom, culminating in Absalom's attempt to depose his father as ruler.

Yes, David was forgiven, but did he get away with his sins? Hardly. Even though David was forgiven, he forever had scars from his unhealthy choices. When we forgive, we are not endorsing unhealthy behavior. To the contrary, we are demonstrating the only healthy response.

Myth 4: Forgiveness Leads to Greater Vulnerability

Many of my patients have been seriously wronged, abused, and assaulted. In response, they develop great resentment and anger. The anger makes them feel strong and less vulnerable. The idea of not having such anger and rage can feel like a loss of power, with subsequent increased vulnerability.

But does forgiveness really increase vulnerability? If those who were assaulted forgave their assailants, does that mean they would fail to take precautions, such as locking doors or avoiding strange places at night? Of course not. In reality, such individuals are generally less vulnerable, because they have become more sensitized and, therefore, are more alert and take more precautions.

Additionally, those who cling to bitterness and refuse to forgive are emotional time bombs waiting to go off at the slightest touch. They easily react with anger, often misread innocent events as offensive, and see insults where none are intended. Such oversensitivity results in less self-control and greater susceptibility to provocation.

Imagine that you have just returned from lying out at the beach, but unfortunately you seriously overdid it and have a severe sunburn. What would you do if your child jumped on your back or your spouse gave you a big hug? Might you instinctively push them away? Or might you have a reflexive feeling of anger or irritation? How much more so if someone purposely slapped your shoulders? But a few days later, after the sunburn has subsided, if your child jumps on your back or your spouse gives you a hug, how do you respond? When we forgive, we heal the emotional sunburns in our hearts and enable ourselves to engage in many more experiences without pain or irritation.

Myth 5: Forgiveness Means Restored Trust

As we saw in Kate's experience, forgiving someone does not change that person. Trust is based on the trustworthiness of the individual. Forgiveness is a change of heart attitude for the victim, not the assailant, and results in the injured person's relinquishing any demand for vengeance. In no way, however, does it restore trust. Not until the offending parties demonstrate that they are trustworthy can trust be reestablished.

Myth 6: Forgiveness Means Forgetting

This one is a little tricky because, in a certain sense, forgiveness does mean forgetting. However, such forgetting does not involve memory erasure.

Can you remember a time that one of your children told you a fib and you had to discipline the child? Did they repent and ask forgiveness? And did you forgive them? Now that forgiveness, repentance, and reconciliation have occurred, do you think *Here comes that little liar of mine* the next time you see your child come running toward you? Of course not. When reconciliation occurs, the transgression is forgotten *as far as the relationship is concerned* because it is no longer relevant to the relationship. But is memory erased? Are the facts of what took place lost from history? No. This type of forgetting can safely occur only after reconciliation. To forget before the person who has offended has repented would open oneself up to unnecessary risk.

This myth also stems from misunderstandings about how God handles situations. In the Bible God states that if we repent, He will remember our sins no more (see Jer. 31:34; Heb. 8:12; 10:17). Many well-meaning people have taken such passages to indicate that those in heaven have no memory of the sins and mistakes of the righteous, that the recorded sins of the righteous have been erased and vanished from recollection. Let's use our reason to explore this possibility and see if it withstands scrutiny.

We have already mentioned David's sin with Bathsheba—that he repented and was forgiven—yet we still have a record of it to read. If it has been erased from memory in heaven, does that mean that, when we are reading our Bibles here on earth, God does not allow our guardian angels to look over our shoulders?

Consider the time that David, Bathsheba, and Uriah meet in heaven and Solomon joins them. Will David and Bathsheba know that Solomon is their son? Will Uriah remember that Bathsheba was his wife? Will Uriah have any questions for David and Bathsheba? Will any of them have memories of their lives on earth?

Many people have a problem with retaining our memories in heaven because they are afraid of how others will treat them because of what they did on earth. They don't believe that anyone could love them and be kind to them if others know of their scarlet past. Let's look at some evidence from Scripture.

Consider the story of the woman caught in adultery and brought before Jesus. We all recognize that Jesus didn't condemn her, and we can take courage in knowing that He won't condemn us, either. But consider those who brought the woman to Jesus. His enemies, they had been plotting His death and eventually crucified Him. Now they brought the woman in an attempt to trap Him.

If Christ would have encouraged those gathered to stone the adulterous woman, they would have accused Him before the Romans as usurping Roman authority, because only the Roman government could sentence someone to death. Or had He urged the woman's release, they would have presented Him before the people as undermining the law of Moses.

Jesus recognized that they had set up the situation to entrap Him. He knew that they were His enemies; He knew their secret sins also. Consequently He could have chosen to expose their sins and then urged the crowd to turn against them. Instead, He followed a much different path—one that the religious leaders had not anticipated. Bending down, He began to trace their various sins on the paving stones of the Temple court—without names. Each person observed his own shortcoming, felt convicted, turned, and left.

Isn't it amazing that Jesus protected the reputations of even His enemies! If God guards their reputations, how much more will He those of His friends?

Here we have concrete evidence that God demonstrated at great expense to Himself how He operates His universe. In heaven memory will continue, but no one will use the information in destructive ways. Our recollections of even tragic events will serve to enhance further our love and appreciation for God and His methods. Such remembering will protect the universe from rebellion ever arising again.

What about Judas? Jesus knew that the disciple planned to betray Him, but He didn't expose him to the disciples. In fact, when Judas left the upper room on his way to the Temple officials, the other disciples thought he was going to buy needed items or minister to the poor.

With God there is no forgetting of the history of our lives. But because we have been healed and our hearts are in harmony with His, as far as the relationship is concerned it is forgotten. God doesn't bring it up—it is no longer an issue.

Consider what would happen if your child underwent months of painful and miserable treatments for leukemia. It has depressed the child's immune system, and he or she is weak and frequently nauseated. His or her hair falls out. Would you treat this child differently from your other children? Would you provide greater care, take greater precautions, and seek greater involvement?

But if the leukemia is in complete and total remission, and your child is well, would you still surround the child with all the restrictions and special precautions? And would you ever forget the history of your child's brush with death? Of course not. But as far as how the child is treated, after being eliminated the leukemia is forgotten. It no longer matters, and no precautions are needed. This is how it is with God and us. After we are healed, we no longer need the special precautions. But we still remember the history of our illness, and it adds to our appreciation of God for the special efforts He devoted to us.

God forgets our sins in the same way a parent forgets the leukemia her child once had. Sin is no longer part of our character and therefore is no longer relevant in our relationship with Him.

Myth 7: Forgiving Means That the Guilty Person Gets Away With It

The final and perhaps the most difficult myth to recognize and resolve is that forgiving someone means that they escape any responsibility or consequences for what they have done. This myth is the most difficult for my patients to recognize. It involves misconceptions about God, the problem with sin, and His solution for it.

In reality, no one ever gets away with sin because, as we have repeatedly seen, we actually damage ourselves when we sin (act destructively). With every unhealthy act—and even every unhealthy thought that we cherish—we make ourselves increasingly hard-hearted, selfish, and evil.

Some people fail to see that the problem with sin is that it damages the sinner. Instead, they believe that someone who sins must suffer an imposed penalty. When no penalty exists, they have difficulty forgiving, because it seems as if no one is holding the sinner accountable. The correct understanding of sin, however, allows for the recognition that no one ever gets away with it—rather, those who sin slowly destroy themselves.

Toni was distressed, angry, and irritable. Her anger was the result of conflict with a coworker who frequently spent hours on the phone talking to family and friends and did very little work. Although her coworker's negligence did not place more work upon Toni, she became increasingly preoccupied with the perceived injustice. "It just isn't fair," she summarized. "I work hard and don't get to talk on the phone all day." Toni was disturbed because she didn't understand the nature of sin.

To help her deal with the situation, I asked her to consider the following scenario. If she agreed to wash someone's car for $50, accepted the $50, but didn't wash the car, how would she feel? "Awful, like a thief," Toni immediately answered. She recognized that her self-esteem and self-worth would fall, and shame, guilt, depression, and anxiety would increase.

Next I asked how she would feel if she agreed to perform certain duties for a prescribed wage, accepted the pay, but didn't perform her duties. When Toni didn't seem to make the connection, I posed this question: If her husband didn't brush his teeth, would she think he was getting a better deal? She realized that such a thing was not possible, because his teeth would eventually decay. That's the point: The coworker who cheated the boss was decaying something far more valuable than teeth—she was destroying her soul. The point became obvious to Toni. She was able to see that her coworker was not getting a better deal, but in fact was damaging herself.

Misunderstandings about God and His forgiveness have circulated for centuries. George MacDonald, the famous nineteenth-century theologian, confronted these very same issues:

"The Lord never came to deliver men from the consequences of their sins while those sins yet remained. . . . Yet, feeling nothing of the dread hatefulness of their sin, men have constantly taken this word that the Lord came to deliver us from our sins to mean that he came to save them from the punishment of their sins.

"This idea has terribly corrupted the preaching of the gospel. The message of the good news has not been truly communicated. Unable to believe in the forgiveness of the Father in heaven, imagining him not at liberty to forgive, or incapable of forgiving forthright; not really believing him God who is fully our Savior, but a God bound—either in his own nature or by a law above him and compulsory upon him—to exact some recompense or satisfaction for sin, a multitude of religious teachers have taught their fellow men that Jesus came to bear our punishment and save us from hell. But in that they have misrepresented his true mission."*

The issue that God is trying to accomplish in our lives is the actual healing and transformation of our hearts and minds, here and now. It involves much more than simple forgiveness. As we learn how to forgive others, we cooperate with God for the healing of our own minds.

If this is still a little confusing, consider the case of the serial killer Jeffrey Dahmer, who murdered numerous people, dismembered their bodies, and put them in his refrigerator. Although Mr. Dahmer is deceased, let's assume that he is still alive and that the president forgives, pardons, and sets him free. Would you want Jeffrey Dahmer as your next-door neighbor? Why not? After all, he would be forgiven. But would he be changed? Would he be safe to live next door to? Or would he have so twisted himself that he is unsafe for you to accept as a neighbor? Here is the ultimate question in the problem with sin. Sin has damaged us, and only those who have cooperated with God for the restoration of His image within will be saved.

The Bible speaks of this transformation in a variety of ways: as being re-created in the inner person, as having the mind of Christ, as having God's law written on our heart and mind, as walking by the Spirit and not the flesh, as having circumcision of the heart by the Spirit, as being a new creation, and as being reborn. All of the metaphors point to the same thing: being changed, healed, restored; having the damage of sin healed; having selfishness replaced with the law of love and liberty; having an ennobled reason and pure conscience directing a stable will in the establishment and maintenance of self-control; being one with God in method, principle, and motive; and operating from the law of love and liberty.

In the aftermath of the terrorist attacks on September 11, 2001, many people yearn for a safe society. They want a place where they don't have to be afraid, where they don't need security guards patrolling with rifles, and where everyone can be trusted. This is exactly why only those who have cooperated with God for transformation of heart will enter heaven. Heaven will include only those who are safe, who can be trusted. Only those who have recovered the ability to be self-controlled and self-governing will be able to handle the absolute freedoms in God's universe. Forgiving others is one of the steps we take in cooperating with Him for our own healing and transformation.

---

* George MacDonald, *Discovering the Character of God* (Minneapolis: Bethany House, 1989), p. 39.

CHAPTER 13

The Casualties of War

I n the aftermath of the terrorist attacks against the World Trade Center and Pentagon on September 11, 2001, many of my patients have asked, "Why does God let such things happen?" "Why do bad things happen to good people?" "Why doesn't God protect the innocent?" During the national prayer service for the victims of the September 11 attack Billy Graham posed the same questions and indicated that he was still looking for answers.

Again I can see the face of my patient in the preface and hear Her cry. Once more I find myself haunted by Her pain and Her desperate search for answers to such questions. It reminds me of my inability to provide Her meaningful answers. And now I wish I could find Her and tell Her these truths.

Why Does a Loving God Allow So Much Pain?

In his anger Frank radiated an undercurrent of seething rage that seemed about to erupt like a volcano at the slightest provocation, an illusion reinforced by his red hair and face. As his anger rose, his face reddened like a thermometer.

At six feet two inches and weighing 350 pounds, he tended to be somewhat intimating to those around him. Because his angry outbursts often caused him great problems at work, his employer suggested that Frank seek help dealing with his anger in order to avoid losing his job.

When he first visited me, Frank was guarded and reluctant to open up. After several sessions, however, he painfully disclosed that his uncle had molested him when he was 6 years old. Since that time, confused about his sexuality and wondering if he were gay, he had struggled to find himself. Such doubt had led to his hating himself and constantly ridiculing himself in his own mind.

So offensive was the possibility that he was gay that he repeatedly stated he would prefer to kill himself rather than pursue such a lifestyle. Frank loathed himself for having such confused feelings and was angry with God for allowing him to be abused. He blamed the Lord for the confusion over his sexuality and struggled to find some answers as to why He would allow innocent children to suffer.

His hatred toward God and himself was so severe that he had developed a cynical attitude, trusting no one and ridiculing everyone. Constantly finding fault with others, he responded with irritation if anyone attempted to be friendly. He actively pushed most people away, especially if there was any hint of attraction. Though terrified of intimacy, he complained bitterly of his lonely life and his deep craving for a wife and family. The man was confused, hurt, angry, and lost.

We began to explore these issues in light of God's principles of truth, love, and freedom. Frank needed to be able to make sense of his life, to develop an understanding of his situation that was reasonable and healthy and would promote healing. He believed that if God really were love, then He would never allow anyone to abuse children. Whether he realized it or not, he was asking the age-old question: Why does a loving God allow so much pain?

First: A Universal War

The only way to answer that question adequately is to take the largest view possible. We must put the issue in its proper context, which is war. Not a struggle between local governments or even a global conflict. No, this conflict involves the entire universe, and our planet is the battleground. The forces involved have been battling for millennia, and the issues at stake are love, freedom, and individuality. Not fought with power and might or bullets and tanks or flaming swords and lightning bolts, rather it is a battle about two methods, two principles, two motives—between the principles of selfishness and love. It is in the context of this universal conflict that we must look for understanding to these difficult questions.

During World War II the United States sent many of its young men to fight for freedom in Europe and Asia. Did it surprise anyone that many of our soldiers were shot at, wounded, and killed? No one found that unexpected or startling. Thus no one demanded, "Why do bad things keep happening to our troops?" We realized that we were at war with an enemy determined to kill our soldiers.

In a similar way, we on this planet battle an enemy determined to wound and destroy as many of us as he can. The apostle Peter reminds us of our need to be alert: "Be self-controlled and alert. Your enemy the devil prowls around like a roaring lion looking for someone to devour" (1 Peter 5:8).

But while our opponent seeks to destroy us, it is God's goal to save us: "If God is for us, who can be against us?" (Rom. 8:31). But if, in fact, God is on our side, why do bad things still strike His friends? Why does He let it happen? If He is all-powerful, then why does He not intervene to prevent such painful things?

The War Is Not About Power

First, this struggle is not simply a question of who has the most might. Satan has never claimed to have more power than God. The Bible reminds us that the devils believe and tremble (James 2:19). Aware of divine power, Satan knew that it was futile to attempt to overthrow God by force. Therefore, he has sought to turn us away from God by intimating that the Lord abuses His power and that we do not have freedom. As we have seen in earlier chapters, the law of liberty respects individuality. When anything violates the law of liberty, love is destroyed. Satan misrepresents God as abusive in an attempt to instill revulsion against Him, thus erasing love and inciting rebellion.

But God so loved the world that He sent His only Son, not to condemn it but to save it. In other words, He sent his Son to reveal His love for us and thus awaken love in our hearts.

The War Is About Love

Love cannot be won by force. Only by love is love awakened. God sent His Son to demonstrate that even when God's own life is on the line, the principles of love and freedom are too important to violate. Christ would not use His power to save Himself on the cross. Why? Because to do so would prove Satan right: that God is an arbitrary, capricious deity who utilizes His power to manipulate for His own ends. In such a universe love and freedom would not exist.

But Christ revealed just the opposite—that with God we have real freedom. The Lord respects our freedom so much that He would die rather than force us to comply with His way. But with true freedom comes great risks—those of rebellion and abuse.

Only the Healed Will Make Safe Neighbors

In the aftermath of the World Trade Center and Pentagon attacks, with threats of new terrorism daily in the news, people long more than ever for a land free from fear, crime, and the abuse of freedom—a land that will not need armies to chase down terrorists or police to patrol the streets.

Such a place will exist only if it is inhabited by people who have freely chosen to cooperate with God for the healing of their minds. The universe will be safe only when inhabited by individuals who value and practice the methods of love and liberty. Only those who have cooperated with God for the restoration of His image within will be saved, because only those who have been healed will make safe neighbors.

God, therefore, allows individuals to develop their characters here on earth in accordance with the free exercise of individual will. If He were to intervene in someone's mind to force that individual to choose a particular act, then that person would be no longer a free being, but a divinely controlled automaton. Such an individual would be unable to love, and would be limited to carrying out programmed commands. What God wants cannot be achieved by using His might and power. Trust can be restored only by revealing truth, in love, and then leaving people free to conclude for themselves what they should do about it.

Second: Discipline

The law of liberty requires that all must decide for themselves which methods they prefer. It is in the choosing of the right that we cooperate with God for the transformation of our hearts and minds. But all too often we have become so entrenched in unhealthy behaviors or relationships that we are unable to recognize the truth. Therefore, as a good parent, God will discipline those He loves in an attempt to awaken their minds to the danger they are in.

Trials often occur to help us see more clearly the unhealthy things in our lives, so that we might choose to change them. As one of my colleagues has said: "Pain is the fertilizer of the soul." It is during difficult times that we often experience the greatest growth. They reveal our true character and bring our defects to light, giving us the opportunity for healing and growth. Consider the following biblical texts:

"Consider it pure joy, my brothers, whenever you face trials of many kinds, because you know that the testing of your faith develops perseverance. Perseverance must finish its work so that you may be mature and complete, not lacking anything" (James 1:2-4).

"In this you greatly rejoice, though now for a little while you may have had to suffer grief in all kinds of trials. These have come so that your faith—of greater worth than gold, which perishes even though refined by fire—may be proved genuine and may result in praise, glory and honor when Jesus Christ is revealed" (1 Peter 1:6, 7).

"For you, O God, tested us; you refined us like silver" (Ps. 66:10).

"Those whom I love I rebuke and discipline" (Rev. 3:19).

What do these passages mean? Imagine that you've been in an automobile accident and have broken your leg. The doctor has set the bone, and now it's time for physical therapy. What do you think the physical therapy would feel like? Would the healing process involve pain? Now consider a woman who endured sexual abuse as a child and has entered psychotherapy to heal the damage she incurred. Again, would the therapy be painful?

We are sick. Because our minds are defective, we find ourselves drawn to destructive methods of coping and relating. The healing process is painful. But if, after breaking your leg, you engage in physical therapy, will the pain diminish and your strength and autonomy return? If the woman abused as a child works through her abuse in therapy, will the pain also diminish and will her character become healthier?

God understands that healing involves pain. He too suffered pain in order to heal His universe. Without His personal sacrifice He could not restore peace and health to the universe.

Why Did Jesus Have to Die?

But why did God have to make such a sacrifice? How does His pain heal His universe? Why was Christ's death necessary?

Because nothing else could win us back to complete trust while securing the universe from future rebellion. Love cannot be forced. Our love must be freely given.

In order to love God, we must come to know Him. In our fallen state we had lost sight of His true character and methods. Satan's distortions had darkened our minds. Only the revelation of the divine character could remove Satan's misrepresentations. And only one equal to God could accurately reveal that character.

Christ came as God in human flesh to roll back the darkness in which Satan had enveloped the world. The Savior's life and death refute the lies Satan has told about God and vindicate His character and government before humanity and the onlooking universe. "For God was pleased to have all his fullness dwell in him [Christ], and through him to reconcile to himself all things, whether things on earth or things in heaven, by making peace through his blood, shed on the cross" (Col. 1:19, 20).

Christ Himself stated that His mission was to reveal the Father's character to humanity in order to restore God's love in our hearts. In His final prayer to His Father before His crucifixion, Jesus stated, "I have made you known to them, and will continue to make you known in order that the love you have for me may be in them and that I myself may be in them" (John 17:26).

Jesus died to demonstrate that even though God has absolute power, He would never use it to restrict individual liberties—that we have real freedom in His government.

Perhaps you've encountered the adage that power corrupts and absolute power corrupts absolutely. The cross of Christ, however, reveals that God is not corrupt, even though He has absolute power.

Think about this. The all-powerful God, who could use His power to force His way, instead grants us real freedom to make our own choice. He actually respects the individuality and freedom of His intelligent creatures. Could anything be more glorious than this?

The Glory of God

Many people conceive of God's glory as great displays of might, power, and fire, but the Bible teaches that His greatest glory reveals itself in His character. Because we are finite beings, many humans frequently react in fear to our all-powerful God. Unfortunately, this fear often leads to rebellion. Once Satan had made his allegations, God could not win His case through the display of power, which would inevitably result in submission based on terror.

God will never utilize coercive tactics, because they are contrary to His benevolent character. The use of might and power to pressure conformity violates the law of liberty and would result in further rebellion. Such methods belong to Satan. If God employed them, He would ultimately lose His case. Although He has immense power, it is not the source of His glory, because power alone would intimidate, leading us to fear Him and subsequently to destroy our love for Him.

Nineteenth-century theologian George MacDonald made this same point: "What is the deepest in God? His power? No, for power could not make him what we mean when we say God. . . . A being whose essence was only power would be such a negation of the divine that no righteous worship could be offered him: his service must be fear, and fear only."[1]

The power isn't what is most important. Instead, it is the trustworthiness of the One who possesses all the power. It is the demonstration of His character—the character of the One who holds the power—that is the real source of divine glory. For example, although God is all-powerful, He can never be provoked—even in the most abusive and horrendous circumstance—to use His power for self-interest. When humanity fully recognizes this, it will restore trust and regenerate love, and we will then open our hearts and minds to Him for healing and restoration.

The Bible is clear on this issue. The book of Haggai declares that the glory of the second Jewish Temple would be greater than that of Solomon's Temple (Haggai 2:7-9). The prophecy refers to the structure the Jews rebuilt after returning from Babylonian captivity.

But in the book of Ezra we read that the older Levites and family heads who saw the second Temple mourned because it was so small when compared to Solomon's (Ezra 3:12). If the second Temple was smaller than the first, how could it be more glorious? Most Bible students immediately explain that because Jesus walked in the courts of the second Temple His presence made it more glorious.

But in 2 Chronicles we read that when Solomon's Temple was dedicated, the priests could not enter because the brightness of God's glory was too great (2 Chron. 5:13, 14). In other words, God came to both Temples—one in His unveiled splendor; the other in human form—yet Haggai states that the second was the more glorious. Why? Because it was at the second Temple that Christ revealed the character of God. Because it was at the second Temple that Christ showed that He preferred to permit His creatures to abuse Him rather than use His power in selfish ways. At the second Temple Christ demonstrated that we can trust the One who has the power.

When Moses spoke with God on the mountain, asking the Lord to show him His glory, what did God do? He responded to Moses, "I will cause all my goodness to pass in front of you" (Ex. 33:19). Then God passed in front of Moses, proclaiming, "The Lord, the Lord, the compassionate and gracious God, slow to anger, abounding in love and faithfulness, maintaining love to thousands, and forgiving wickedness, rebellion and sin" (Ex. 34:6, 7).

It was at the cross that God presented the greatest demonstration of His character. Through the cross we see indeed that He is gracious, compassionate, forgiving, patient, kind, faithful, and true. The cross reveals that nothing we do can provoke Him to use His immense power in selfish ways. Although He is all-powerful, He is even more gracious. The Creator actually respects the individuality of His intelligent creatures, even if we abuse that individuality and attempt to destroy Him.

This revelation refutes the misrepresentations that Satan has so successfully spread through the universe and particularly on our planet. The depiction of God's character—especially His trustworthiness—wins us back to trust and results in our healing, our salvation.

Third: A Revelation of the Two Antagonistic Motives

What happened at the cross helps explain to some extent why bad things happen to good people. We live on a planet that operates on Satan's principles of survival of the fittest—of self first—and the events of our world illustrate the two great antagonistic motives or methods.

God demonstrates that only in an atmosphere of freedom can love exist, that neither can be forced or coerced. The Lord shows us that with Him we always have real freedom, even though pain might accompany it.

Satan leads us to abuse our freedoms to hurt both others and ourselves, and then he deceives us into believing that it is a result of God's punishment or that He doesn't care or is impotent. But the devil trembles at the prospect that we might actually come to see things as they are. He fears that we might realize that God could not control our actions and still love us at the same time. If He tried, it would destroy love itself.

Freedom is essential for love to exist. It follows that love and freedom risk great injury. The reason God hasn't brought an end to our rebellion from His law of love and liberty is that many here on our planet have not yet understood the issues and made an intelligent decision to accept the healing that He offers. God waits patiently, wanting all to be healed.

The issue at stake is healing the mind by ennobling the reason, cleansing the conscience, strengthening the will, purifying the thoughts, and regaining control of the feelings. It involves the reestablishment of thoughts and actions based on reason, truth, love, and freedom.

God cannot change our hearts and minds by force. Instead, He leaves us free to come to our own conclusion through the revelation of truth spoken in love. Unfortunately, a false gospel prevents this from happening because it represents God in the opposite light. Instead of instilling trust, it plants fear in the human mind.

A False Gospel

One popular religious teaching states that the problem with sin is not found in our unhealthy hearts and minds, but in God's anger and wrath. It also contends that Christ came to die to appease His wrath. Further, it declares that Christ is in heaven pleading to His Father in our behalf so that when we stand in the judgment, God will see, not our sinfulness, but instead Christ's perfect righteousness.

This view often masquerades as a wolf in sheep's clothing through such cherished and beloved phrases as "covered by the blood," "washed in the blood," "covered in the robe of Christ's righteousness," and the like. Far from what it professes, this false view is actually the candy-coated rotten-apple theory. It holds that no heart change is needed; merely cover the rotten heart with the "blood of Christ," and then it *appears* perfect and can pass through the scrutiny of the judgment. As we have already seen, only those who have cooperated with God for actual heart transformation will enter heaven, because without heart change we would not be safe to be around.

Sin Is Like Smallpox

If one of your children came down with smallpox, would you let that child remain in your home with your other children? Or would you want to protect the rest from infection? Should you decide not to let the infected child stay, would that mean you didn't love him or her? Of course not. Would you even be willing to risk your own health by leaving your healthy children at home and going out to provide whatever assistance you could to the sick child?

And if you had antibodies in your blood that would cure the child, but the child refused your blood transfusion, what would happen? Would you kill your child? Would your child die?

Because we are sick and unfit for heaven, God left His heavenly home to bring us the cure—the truth about Himself. If we reject the cure, the result of that choice will be death.

We see this reality revealed in an Old Testament story that occurred after Israel's exodus from Egypt. Shortly after leaving captivity, Miriam and Aaron became jealous of Moses and began to argue about who should be leading the people. God intervened by striking Miriam with leprosy. Miriam had to leave the camp and could not return until she had been healed (Num. 12).

Leprosy is a biblical metaphor for sin. We are leprous with minds that operate on principles in opposition to God's methods. Only those who co-operate with God for their healing will be able to enter the heavenly camp. Such healing is the process of regaining one's individuality, the ability to think and to act free from the domination of our genetic weakness and according to the principles of love, truth, openness, and freedom.

Some misunderstand this reality. Instead of focusing on the Healer and treatment, they concentrate on their own condition. Finding faults within themselves, they doubt their salvation. Many of my patients are consumed with insecurity about their salvation because they continue to recognize defects in themselves. They fail to see that the issue isn't one of past mistakes or even of ongoing struggles, but of participating in the healing process.

The Key Is Staying on the Path of Life

Suppose that you have become sick with pneumonia in both your lungs, and your symptoms include severe fevers, shortness of breath, and ever-diminishing strength. If you do nothing, wouldn't you be on the path toward death?

But if you go to the physician and begin treatment that includes antibiotics, wouldn't you have entered the path of life? Do you expect to become well immediately on the day that you leave the path of death and commence the path of life (started your antibiotics)? Of course not. But does the healing begin on the day you begin antibiotics? And as long as you stay on the path of life (take your antibiotics and keep your doctor appointments), you can safely assume that a healthy outcome is guaranteed.

In the process of recovery from pneumonia, you'll likely encounter more fevers, chills, sweats, and coughing up ugly stuff. Are such symptoms evidence that your condition is getting worse? Or could you actually cough up more phlegm after you start the antibiotics as the medicines begin attacking the infection?

When we enter the path of life and begin working with God for the healing of our mind, along the way we often cough up some noxious things. Defects of character often come out, and mistakes get made. But those mistakes don't indicate loss of salvation. Instead they often represent the struggle against and expulsion of such defects from the character.

Once you begin the antibiotics to treat your pneumonia, if you decide to halt your medicine and no longer visit the doctor, what will happen? After we come to Christ, if we choose to stop walking with Him and stop cooperating with Him for the healing of our mind, what will likely occur?

Physicians don't kill their noncompliant patients, but too often those patients die. God's rebellious and unruly children also perish. Just as the wages of noncompliance with medical treatment is death, so the wages of sin is also death. Both occur as the inevitable consequence of choosing a self-destructive course.

Death comes to the wicked as a consequence of their own violation of the universal principles that govern life—because of persistently ignoring the laws of love and liberty. Remember that both laws are not legislative enactments, but are similar to the law of gravity—a constant reality in the universe. Because of humanity's ignorance about these issues, God has graciously intervened to suspend the reaping of the consequence of breaking the laws of love and liberty, and has instead provided human beings with an opportunity for deliverance.

God Suspends the Consequences for a Time

Imagine yourself atop the Empire State Building. God has said, "In the day that thou jumpeth off the Empire State Building, thou shalt surely die."

Soon Satan, in the form of an eagle (instead of a serpent), comes soaring by and calls God's trustworthiness into question. "Did God really say in the day you jump you will die? Oh, no, you won't. Look at me. I can fly because I jumped. God is only trying to keep you from flying too." So you jump. What a thrill. The air rushes by, the speed builds, and you must certainly be flying. But then you notice that you're going only one way—straight down. Overcome by fear, you realize that if things don't change, you will surely die.

As fear overwhelms you, God suddenly reaches out and stops you in midair. Suspending the consequences, He graciously gives you an opportunity to step through a window and live. He has even sent His Son to be thrown off the building to demonstrate what happens. But this time God restrained Himself and did not suspend the consequences for His Son. And as we hear Christ say, "My God, My God, why have You forsaken Me," we see that instead of reaching an exalted state of existence, the violation of the law of gravity results in death, and as a natural consequence, not an imposed penalty.

But if you persistently tell God to get out of your life, if you repeatedly refuse His entreaties to step through the window and insist on going your own way, He will respect your freedom and let you do as you wish. And when He lets go, you will fall to your death, the natural result of the violation of God's universal law.

God Is Not as His Enemies Have Portrayed

The theory that God is unforgiving and requires appeasement transforms Him into an arbitrary dictator pleased with sacrifices. It creates a disparity between the Father and the Son, particularly when you recall that this theory also depicts Christ as a merciful mediator who pleads to His vengeful Father in an attempt to protect us from the Father's wrath. Those who have refused to surrender their reason have rightly rejected this theory.

Unfortunately, we as Christians have all too often failed to present effectively the truth that God is not like this, leaving many to reject the notion of deity altogether. We have failed to declare the truth that Christ is God's envoy, representative, and ambassador, who brings us the truth about God and His methods and principles. We have left many with the choice of surrendering reason or rejecting God. Given those two choices, many people prefer to reject a deity who would require one to surrender reason, rather than to accept an irrational belief system.

The good news, as articulated in this book, is that God is not like this. He truly respects our individuality, our ability to think and to reason. When we understand this truth and begin to trust such a God, we leave the path of death and enter the path of life. And after we have started on the path of life and cooperated with the Lord for the healing of our minds, there still remains one more reason the righteous suffer.

Fourth: A Witness

The first chapter of the book of Job permits us to view behind the veil to see the war being waged in heaven. The scene begins with God sitting on His throne. Around Him have gathered the sons of the morning, God's intelligent creatures from throughout the universe.

Soon Satan arrives from roaming the earth. Then God does something astounding. He makes a judgment about Job, observing to Satan; "Have you considered my servant Job? He is perfect and righteous in all his ways. There is no one on the earth like him." But Satan responds, "Oh, no, he's not. Job merely pretends to be righteous because You pay well. Take away Your bribes, and we'll see his true character. He will curse You to Your face."

Now the contest begins. Who is telling the truth, God or Satan? The sons of the morning must have had their interest heightened when they heard the Lord declare, "OK, Satan, Job is in your hands. You can do anything you like with him except kill him."

Satan was free to treat Job any way he wanted. And what did he do? He could have given Job 100 times more wealth than he already possessed, but he didn't. Because Satan is the destroyer, he immediately wiped out the man's wealth, children, and health. In doing so, Satan revealed to the onlooking universe that he—not God—is the destroyer. Why would the Lord allow such a thing?

Many people assume that Job's story serves as an illustration for how the righteous endure suffering. More accurately, it concerns the universal war between good and evil. Angels cannot read hearts and minds. If they could, Satan would never have deceived one third of them during the first conflict in heaven. When God declared Job righteous, Satan contended otherwise. The angels could not determine who was telling the truth. If Job were to yield to Satan's temptation to curse God, then Satan could turn to the onlooking universe and declare, "See, I told you. God was wrong about Job, and He's wrong about me. You can't trust what He says."

The issues at stake in the book of Job are enormous. But Job was such a trusted friend of God that God could call this human being to the witness stand of the universe to say what is right about Him. *Sometimes* the righteous suffer as witnesses, demonstrating the difference between the two antagonistic motives: God's methods of love and liberty and Satan's ways of selfishness, force, and coercion.

God Offers True Freedom

God's government offers true freedom. He allows individuals to exercise their will for good or for evil openly, thus revealing to all—both the onlooking universe and us—what happens when one prefers Satan's methods to God's.

As we have seen in the lives of many of the patients discussed in this book, when God's methods get ignored, pain and destruction occur. The Lord allows such painful events to happen because He truly does provide freedom. At the same time, however, the abuse of our freedom reveals the difference between God's methods and Satan's.

God wants us to see the way of health, the way of life, the way of love and liberty, and then freely choose His methods and live. It is only by the free exercise of our will to choose the truth that we recover from the problems that trouble us.

It is true that we do not in ourselves possess the power to free ourselves from sin. But when we exercise the will and freely choose what is right, God imbues the mind with divine energy that provides the strength necessary to break free from destructive patterns of living. As the apostle Peter said, we become "partakers of the divine nature" and live in harmony with God and His methods (2 Peter 1:4, KJV). Then we become true soldiers of Christ, willing to be wounded, if necessary, in order to reveal the truth and win the war.

My friend Graham Maxwell stated it this way: "I believe that the most important of all Christian beliefs is the one that brings joy and assurance to God's friends everywhere—the truth about our heavenly Father that was confirmed at such cost by the life and death of his Son.

"God is not the kind of person His enemies have made Him out to be—arbitrary, unforgiving and severe. . . . God is just as loving and trustworthy as His Son, just as willing to forgive and heal. Though infinite in majesty and power, our Creator is an equally gracious person who values nothing higher than the freedom, dignity, and individuality of His intelligent creatures—that their love, their faith, their willingness to listen and obey, may be freely given. He even prefers to regard us not as servants but as friends. This is the truth revealed through all the books of Scripture. This is the everlasting good news that wins the trust and admiration of God's loyal children throughout the universe.

"Like Abraham and Moses—the ones God spoke of as His trusted friends—God's friends today want to speak well and truly of our heavenly Father. We covet as the highest of all commendations the words of God about Job: 'He has said of Me what is right.'"[2]

I wonder what my patient in the preface would have said if I would have shared these truths with Her. How would She have responded if She had realized that God hadn't abused Her? How would She feel to know that God Himself had suffered in order to reach Her? And how would it have changed Her life to discover that He wanted to heal Her? I think that She would have been relieved and glad. Most important of all, I think She would have liked such a God.

---

[1] George MacDonald, "The Creation in Christ," *Unspoken Sermons, Third Series* (London: Longmans, Green and Co., 1889).

[2] A. Graham Maxwell, "What We Believe." At www.pineknoll.org/index.html.

CHAPTER 14

The Way of Death

"There is a way that seems right to a man,
but in the end it leads to death."—Prov. 14:12, NIV.

As we have repeatedly discovered, the problem with sin is that it destroys. Violations of God's law of love and liberty naturally result in damage to our ability to reason and think. We lose the ability to discern what is healthy from the unhealthy, what is right from wrong.

When we choose destructive behavior, we gradually weaken the conscience so that it is no longer sensitive to the breaking of God's law of love and liberty. Losing our moral bearing, we become like unthinking animals driven by passion and lust.

If we persist in rebellion, we become so damaged that no amount of truth will make an impact, because sin has irrevocably destroyed the faculties of reason and conscience. Satan's goal is to destroy our higher mental faculties, dethrone reason, distort or destroy conscience, and control the will with the passions and feelings. It is the way of death.

When the faculties of the mind that respond to truth have perished, God can no longer do anything to save us. We are beyond His reach, and He will sadly let us go to reap the consequences of our choice. He lets us follow the path of death.

Truth Enters the Mind Through Reason and Conscience

Christ said, "The truth will set you free" (John 8:32). But having no truth of his own, Satan does everything in his power to prevent God's truth from reaching our understanding. He does this in several ways. First, he attempts to destroy reason and conscience, because it is through them alone that truth enters the mind. Without reason and conscience we are incapable of understanding truth and are, therefore, helpless in our fight for freedom.

Mutually Exclusive Beliefs Destroy Reason

One of the methods Satan uses to destroy reason is to convince people to believe things that are antithetical and that don't make sense. To achieve his goal, he influences them to disregard their reason so that they accept two things that cannot be true at the same time.

For example, Satan counters the truth that God is love by encouraging us to believe that He chooses who will be saved and who will be lost, insisting that we have no free choice in the matter. As we have previously seen, love *cannot* exist without freedom. Therefore, the two beliefs are mutually exclusive. Both cannot be true at the same time, and the only way to believe both is to surrender reason. In such a situation we rationalize the contradiction by saying, "I take that on faith," which, as we have seen, isn't faith at all.

The Youth Pastor and the Marshmallow Man

A youth pastor did his best to depict the wonders of heaven as he conducted a weekend seminar. He gave a glorious description of the unimaginable delights awaiting us in heaven and God's never-ending love for us. Then, in sudden contrast, he displayed a marshmallow man suspended from a string. As he set the marshmallow man afire, the youth pastor described in horrible detail the pain and suffering God would inflict on all those who refused to be saved. He told the young people that the Lord has gone to enormous lengths to demonstrate His love for us, but if we refuse to surrender our lives to Him, He will be forced to torture and destroy.

But the youth minister's demonstration presents an antithetical belief. If we utilize our reason, we would realize that God cannot be the loving Father and the threatening destroyer at the same time. If He dealt with us through intimidating methods, then our response to Him would be coerced rather than freely given. Such a relationship cannot be true because it would violate God's law of liberty and would result in rebellion. One can believe the youth minister's position only by dethroning reason.

When the Life-giver Lets Go . . .

If God is not threatening to destroy the unrepentant, then what will He do to those who reject Him? It is very simple, really. He takes the only loving action He can: He lets them go, and when the Life-giver lets go, they die.

Consider a husband who comes home from work and is devastated when his wife tells him that she is leaving him for another man. How might the husband respond?

What if he grabbed her, dragged her to the basement, handcuffed her to the wall, put a gun to her head, and said, "All I want is your love. But if you refuse to love me, I'll be forced, by my love, to kill you"? How would she react? Would she feel greater love or a greater desire to get away?

Such treatment clearly violates the law of liberty and results in greater rebellion, not greater love. Since the husband cannot win his wife with such tactics, what can he do? Asking her to stay, he can demonstrate his love for her in actions and deeds. He can even have an envoy go to his wife and try to convince her to stay. But if, after all his efforts, she insists on leaving him, what's the only loving and just route that he can take? Let her go.

If we insist on leaving God, despite all His efforts to win us back, the only loving and just thing He can do is release us. And when the Life-giver does that, we die.

God's letting go, His giving us up to reap the consequence of our choice, is what the Bible refers to as His wrath. In Romans 1 Paul states three times (verses 24, 26, and 28) that God's wrath is "giving them up." When I first considered this possibility, it was very difficult for me to accept, because I had been taught my entire life that God would one day use His power to punish and destroy. The Flood, Sodom and Gomorrah, the deaths of the firstborn of Egypt, and many other such stories in the Old Testament supported the idea that God would punish. The popular doctrine of an eternal hell teaches that God will punish forever.

But what I didn't understand then was what God actually said to Adam and Eve: "If you eat the fruit of the tree in the middle of the garden, *you will die*" (see Gen. 2:17). In other words, He said, "Should you disobey, your actions will so change you that it will result in your death. If you insist on leaving Me, I will let you go. And since I am the source of your life, when you separate from Me, you will perish. The natural consequence of violating My law of love and liberty is self-destruction."

I had also forgotten that only one Person in all history has died the death God told Adam and Eve about, the death that is the wages of sin and that results from separation from God—the sinners' death. All the examples that I had previously used to understand this (the Flood, Sodom and Gomorrah, the firstborn of Egypt) didn't apply, because every one of those people will one day be resurrected, either in the resurrection of life or that of damnation (Matt. 5:28, 29; Rev. 20:4-6).

I had to look to the cross and discover what had happened to Christ. I had to see how God treated the One who became sin, though He knew no sin (see 2 Cor. 5:21). On the cross God treated His Son as an unrepentant, unhealable sinner.

Christ took the sinner's place on the cross and experienced from the Father what the unrepentant will ultimately endure at the final judgment. And what did God do to His Son at the cross? What did Christ plead? "My God, My God, why are You torturing Me? beating Me? raining fire down from heaven on Me?" No! "My God, My God, why have You forsaken Me, abandoned Me, given Me up?" (see Matt. 27:46; Rom. 4:25).

The evidence supports, and it is extremely reasonable to believe, that a loving God will release those who freely choose to separate from Him. He allows them to leave because they have persisted in rebellion so long that they are beyond healing. Through refusing to use the faculties that respond to truth, they have destroyed themselves. They are not the victims of an angry and vengeful God who wants to torture them for all eternity.

Satan's Mass Fraud

Satan is such a convincing liar that he has perpetrated a mass fraud on most of Christianity about this issue. Isaiah 33:14 tells us that "the sinners in Zion are terrified; trembling grips the godless: 'Who of us can dwell with the consuming fire? Who of us can dwell with everlasting burning?'" Many Christians conclude that the passage has hell in mind.

But who does the Bible say will actually dwell there? The next verse answers: "He who walks righteously and speaks what is right, who rejects gain from extortion and keeps his hand from accepting bribes, who stops his ears against plots of murder and shuts his eyes against contemplating evil" (verse 15).

Should we simply approach the passage on "faith"? "God said it. I believe it. That settles it." Or should we ask some questions?

If we take the Bible as a whole, starting in Genesis and searching all the way through, we discover something most interesting. In Exodus 3, when God spoke to Moses from the bush, the bush burned. Then in Exodus 24:16, when God appeared on Sinai, the glory of the Lord looked like a "consuming fire" (verse 17).

Second Chronicles 5:13, 14 tells us that when Solomon's Temple was dedicated, God came down and the priests couldn't enter the Temple because of the brightness of His glory. Ezekiel 28 declares that before his fall Lucifer walked among the *fiery* stones of God's presence (verse 14).

Second Thessalonians 1 declares that the brightness of Christ's coming annihilates the wicked. First Timothy 6:16 describes God as living in unapproachable light. Hebrew 12:29 announces that "our God is a consuming fire." And in Revelation 21:23 we learn that the new heaven and new earth will have no need for the sun and moon to light the earth because God's presence will be its light. What does all this mean?

Satan's great fraud—the one that the vast majority of Christians have accepted—is that the place you don't want to go to and the place you don't want to be is the place of eternal burnings and consuming fire. *But that place is God's very presence.* The righteous bask in God's glory, but it is destructive to the wicked.

God's life-giving glory consumes all who are out of harmony with Him, but heals all who are in harmony. His life-giving glory will transform the righteous, as it did Moses when he was on the mountain in God's presence. When Moses came down from Sinai, he radiated God's glory so much that the Israelites begged him to wear a veil because they couldn't bear to look at him (Ex. 34:35).

Christ demonstrated the same reality just prior to His crucifixion. On His way to the cross Jesus revealed that the fire is not what destroys. He walked through the consuming fire and eternal burning at the Mount of Transfiguration. There, God's fiery glory enveloped Christ. And what happened? Did the fire burn Christ? Was He hurt? No! Because Christ was without sin, the fire was harmless. Christ revealed that the fire is not destructive. It is sin that destroys. It is sin that annihilates the sinner.

The truth presented in Scripture is simple. God gives all free will. If we choose to reject His methods, we slowly destroy our ability to reason, blind our conscience, and lose the ability to govern ourselves. We come to prefer methods of selfishness, force, exploitation, deceit, and secrecy instead of those of truth, love, openness, and freedom. In the process we take ourselves so out of harmony with God that His presence becomes a consuming fire. But those who have cooperated with Him for the restoration of His image within—operating again from principles of love, truth, openness, and freedom—are transformed by His presence and will live forever in His life-giving glory, the eternal burnings and consuming fire.

God Wants Us to Believe Based on Evidence

We encounter many beliefs in Christianity that are mutually exclusive and contribute to the destruction of reason and conscience. God doesn't want us to accept anything for which He hasn't given us sufficient evidence, evidence that appeals to our reason. To believe without evidence is unreasonable and can be done only when reason has been dethroned.

But mutually exclusive beliefs are not the only way to destroy reason and conscience. One of Satan's greatest achievements is to get Christians to teach as virtuous those activities that dethrone reason. I had the opportunity to experience just such an event up close and personal.

Three Days of Confusion

Several years ago I was invited to attend a weekend seminar sponsored by an interdenominational group of Christians. I have always enjoyed fellowship with other Christians but the aura of secrecy around this event made me cautious.

Before I describe the methods employed during this weekend, I must state that it is my belief that those who ran the weekend did not fully understand what they were doing. The local organizers were a sincere group of Christians who were kind, polite, enthusiastic, and friendly. But they did not establish the procedures the seminar would employ. Instead, they simply followed the guidelines established by a parent organization. Therefore, I believe they never really thought through the significance of what they were doing.

Everyone involved in that weekend, I am fully convinced, was sincere in his or her desire to work for the uplifting of Jesus Christ. Yet sincerity is not always sufficient.

Before his Damascus road experience, Saul of Tarsus sincerely sought to win converts back to Judaism, but he employed methods of force and intimidation. When Paul evangelized for Christ following his Damascus road encounter with Christ, he wrote Romans 14, in which he offers this opinion regarding religious matters: "Let all be fully convinced in their own minds" (Rom. 14:5, NRSV). Paul had learned that God's method involves truth that is spoken in love and that leaves others free to come to their own conclusion. Any method that erodes individual freedom to think and to choose ultimately wars against God, regardless of how sincere the person utilizing it may be.

The stated agenda of the weekend was to enhance one's relationship and walk with God, while building unity among Christian brothers—a goal I heartily support. But even before the meetings began, concerns developed in my mind. To my questions about what was planned, I received evasive answers or was urged not to ask and instead encouraged just to wait and see.

Their ambiguity troubled me because I knew that God operates through an open government. I remembered the first chapter of Job, in which God conducted His business with the entire universe watching. And I thought of Jesus' response during His trial before the Sanhedrin when the high priest questioned Him about His work: "'I have spoken openly to the world,' Jesus replied. 'I always taught in synagogues or at the temple, where all the Jews come together. I said nothing in secret'" (John 18:20).

I knew that God encourages openness and inquiry, because when you have the truth on your side, you have nothing to hide. I also realized that Satan utilizes secrecy and evasion. Because he has no truth, he has to hide as much as he can.

But my friends and those I were acquainted with in the seminar were good, decent, loving people, and I was convinced that they had no ill motives. So I brushed aside my concerns about the secrecy and went ahead with plans to attend.

This particular seminar was organized with very specific rules that were applied quite rigidly. The men were secreted away one weekend, followed by women the next. The participants boarded buses and rode approximately 60 miles to an abandoned school in a remote area utilized for such retreats. The participants could not bring their cars, cell phones, or beepers.

After they arrived, they had to put aside their wristwatches. Then they had to follow a highly structured schedule and were expected to complete specific tasks and fulfill explicit requirements. Regimented group activities included such assignments as random pairing for one-on-one prayer. In addition, participants received a handbook that included specified recitations, verses, and mantras, which everyone had to recite before every meeting.

The mealtimes were controlled, and sleep was regulated. Because they had no watches, many soon lost their sense of time. In fact, their biological clocks soon got out of kilter. They also had their individual space taken away from them. Participants bunked in a barracks-like setting with 20 persons to a room and shared bathrooms. Those running the seminar never allowed anyone to be alone or be provided time for solitary study and reflection.

The staff divided everyone into specified groups and assigned them to tables seating eight to 10 individuals. Although the group assumed that everyone sharing their table was a fellow participant, two of those placed at each table were undercover staff members. The staff members sought to direct the flow of the conversation in the direction the organizers had determined was best, leading the participants to believe they were discussing things among themselves when in actuality they were talking with members of the staff.

The seminar organizers justified the subtle deception by telling the undercover staff members, "If anyone asks you if you are staff, do not lie." But the seminar took great efforts to make it appear that such individuals were in fact participants, so that no one would raise the issue.

This misrepresentation of staff as participants allowed for trust to develop on false pretenses and placed the participants in a position of greater vulnerability to the suggestions introduced by the undercover personnel. The seminar had designed the situation so as to break through any potential resistance offered by individuals and to be able to shape their beliefs from within a perceived circle of trust.

The very spiritual, Bible-based, yet intellectually unchallenging sermon-like presentations further masked what the organizers were doing. The whole environment confused me because I was accustomed to examining doctrines and teachings for any potential danger. But when I examined the content of the presentations at the retreat, I found very little to criticize.

Because I focused on the testimonies and sermonettes, which were generally quite uplifting and inspiring, I failed to see the larger process more clearly. In fact, the methods were so subtle that only after several years of study and reflection have I been able to identify the unhealthy methods employed.

To further confuse and distract, the organizers filled the weekend with gifts and presents of all kinds—food, cards, letters, and multiple symbols of Christ's love, such as doves, nails, or crosses. From what appeared a seemingly never-ending supply, they poured the gifts upon us with the explanation that they demonstrated God's never-ending love.

But further insight has reminded me that God does not utilize methods of secrecy, misdirection, misrepresentation, and control—all masked by superficial kindness and token gifts.

The weekend had been organized to exert extreme group pressure on individuals to achieve conformity without their consent. For instance, the retreat never informed anyone what the agenda would be. Each event was a surprise. No one had the opportunity to consider whether they wanted to participate in an activity prior to finding themselves in the middle of it. By then it was difficult to withdraw, as leaving would create a scene and cause a disturbance. The group pressure ensured conformity. Moreover, if someone did decide to skip an activity, two or three staff members followed after them to persuade them to return. The organizers made every effort to prevent participants from having any time alone.

As I reflect on the experience, I realize that these methods are similar to those used in cults to break down individual thought and to instill group conformity. Such methods are designed to undermine individual identity and the use of reason and conscience. Instead, they promote surrendering individual choice to the group, so that the group can think for the individual. This is destructive, no matter how Christlike in appearance and no matter how sincere the organizers. I think again of Saul before the Damascus road. He was sincere in his desire to please God, yet the methods he used were actually satanic and persecuted Christ. It was when Paul changed his methods that he became a powerful force for God's cause.

The participants constantly found themselves confronted with decisions, but nothing related to what was right or wrong. Most decisions required participants to choose between behavior that would maintain group acceptance or would result in group rejection.

For the last event of the weekend, everyone got herded hastily into a room overcrowded with previous graduates of such seminars. They were told that each of them in turn would go before the audience and be required to share with the group their personal reflection of what the weekend had meant to them. Not offered an opportunity to decline, they would have had to make a considerable scene to avoid giving a public testimony.

Additionally, several hundred people waited with clear expectations of what would be an acceptable testimony, further undermining the ability to present a report free of coercion and intimidation.

When the law of liberty is violated, one of the predictable consequences is rebellion. But those at the seminar displayed no hostility or anger. No evidence of discord or rebellion surfaced. If the law of liberty was violated, then why did no obvious rebellion result? This is where the deception becomes extremely subtle and, therefore, all the more dangerous.

Every participant with whom I spoke *did* experience a desire to rebel, to resist, and to withdraw. Some were clearly more uncomfortable than others, but everyone apparently experienced it.

But because the external trappings were overwhelmingly Christian, the participants were encouraged to assume that their resistance was rebellion against the Holy Spirit. This justification, of course, was far from the truth. The members involved in the weekend seminar came because they wanted to pursue a relationship with the Lord. When the seminar employed methods of secrecy, deception, control, and group pressure, however, each participant had a healthy, God-given reaction to rebel against such tactics. Because the methods were so well cloaked in Christian garb, it was virtually impossible to identify exactly what they wanted to resist. This inability to identify the true nature of the rebellion (against unhealthy methods, not God) left them open to the deception that any resistance was actually against God.

Both the designated and undercover staff fostered and encouraged this misdirection, so the participants were easily convinced to suppress their pursuit of freedom and instead conform to the group ideal. Consequently, the weekend produced no open rebellion, just a slow erosion of individuality and an impaired ability to reason and to think.

The organizers of the weekend, no doubt, intended as their agenda to spread the gospel and increase Christian love. But they were unsuccessful because—even though the weekend was filled with Christian music, prayer, sacraments, and testimonies—they utilized methods of secrecy, manipulation, deceit, coercion, and control.

The gospel (good news) about God is that He doesn't employ such methods. His methods of openness, truth, love, and freedom result in the restoration of the image of God within, the strengthening of reason, the cleansing of the conscience, the development of self-governance, and an increase in liberty and autonomy. But the methods followed by the organizers of the seminar, rather than promoting healing of the mind, unfortunately resulted in the further destruction of the image of God within, as the weekend violated individual freedoms and subtly eroded individual identity.

Symbols Have Meaning

How is it possible for intelligent people to hold beliefs that are mutually exclusive? One of Satan's strategies is to persuade people to accept symbolism as fact rather than to pursue the meaning of the symbols themselves, to accept metaphor as reality rather than to explore the significance of the metaphor.

Christianity is filled with symbols and difficult language that promote the acceptance of beliefs that don't make sense. Consider the word "justification." Ask a pastor what it means, and you'll likely receive an explanation something like the following:

"When the human race sinned, it fell under the condemnation of God's law. The penalty for breaking divine law is death. But God loved us so much that He didn't want us to die, so He sent His Son to pay the price by the shedding of His blood. If you accept the payment of Christ's blood shed in your behalf, then you are justified, or accepted by God. You are washed in the blood, and your sins are pardoned, based not on your works, but on the merits of Christ's payment."

Is this what justification means? Under the format menu on my word processing software is a command, "justify," which I can use to straighten the margins. When I hit that command, guess what happens? The left and right margins come into line. Everything that was out of harmony is put in harmony, everything out of order is put in order, everything out of line is put in line, everything that is wrong is put right. In our world of sin, what is out of order that needs to be put back in order? What is wrong that needs to be set right?

When Adam sinned, did God experience a change in some way so that He now needed to be fixed? Of course not. God is the same yesterday, today, and tomorrow. Then do we need Christ to die to appease God, to change the Father's attitude toward us, to get Him to pardon and forgive? No! "For God so loved the world that he gave his one and only Son" (John 3:16). "God was in Christ reconciling the world to himself" (2 Cor. 5:19, NEB). "If God is for us, who can be against us?" (Rom. 8:31). Christ said, "Anyone who has seen me has seen the Father" (John 14:9). Christ is an "exact representation" of the Father (Heb. 1:3). There was never a problem with God. He has always been on our side.

But when Adam sinned, did he change? Yes! His mind ceased to operate in healthy ways. No longer trusting God or valuing His methods and principles of governing, he became selfish.

What needed to be put right, set right, was the human heart and mind. *To justify* simply means to restore our hearts and minds into harmony with God's, to be won back to love and trust. But it could happen only through revealing the truth about God in love. Then each person would bear the responsibility individually to weigh and to freely decide to accept or reject this truth.

Many symbols in Christianity are misunderstood and result in the dethronement of reason. Think about what it means to be washed in the blood or cleansed by the blood. Are we really washed in red corpuscles? Obviously not. Then what does the imagery stand for?

Blood is a biblical symbol of life (Lev. 17:11). Christ's life reveals the truth about God and exposes the lies that Satan has told about Him. Those who understand and accept this truth have their minds washed or cleansed from the distortions and misrepresentations about God. Won back to trust in Him, they begin to practice His methods.

What does blood do in the body? It brings life (oxygen and nutrients) and removes death (carbon dioxide and waste). Consider the role of the truth about God, as revealed in the life and death of Christ (the blood of Christ).

It brings life (truth) and removes death (lies). To be washed by the blood means to have the mind restored to health by the truth as revealed in Christ.

Hebrews 2:14 provides further insight into this process: "Since the children have flesh and blood, he [Christ] too shared in their humanity so that by his death he might destroy him who holds the power of death—that is, the devil." Did you know that the devil holds the power of death? What is that power?

John 17:3 provides the answer in Christ's own words: "This is eternal life: that they may know you, the only true God, and Jesus Christ, whom you have sent." If eternal life is knowing God, then what would eternal death be? Not knowing God! Then what is Satan's power? The lies he tells about God, that we believe, that keep us from knowing Him.

The blood of Christ symbolizes the truth revealed in Christ's life and death that destroys the lies of Satan. The truth sets us free. It heals our minds and restores our relationship with the Father.

Within Christianity we find many other examples of misunderstood language and symbolism. Think of some examples familiar to you. Then search for their true meaning.

Six Signs That Reason Is Being Destroyed

Since reason can be dethroned in many ways, let's explore some of the telltale signs that indicate that reason is being removed from its intended role. Below are six common signs that often surface when reason is not engaged.

1. God Said It, I Believe It, That Settles It

Many persons exhibit symptoms that indicate that they have allowed their reason to be sidelined and have lost the ability to think for themselves. Perhaps you've heard someone say, "God said it, I believe it, and that settles it." While it sounds very spiritual and seems like "a way that seems right to a man" (Prov. 14:12), in the end it leads to death, because it dethrones reason and impairs the person's ability to recognize truth. It allows for the belief of anything.

Does God want us to believe simply because He says so? Or does He prefer that we believe because the truth is on His side, and we have come to understand the truth? Anyone can make claims, but only God has the truth. Reflect on the Bible text that declares, "God is love" (1 John 4:8). How do we know that God is love? Because the Bible states, "God is love"? Such a statement is only a claim, and Satan could make a similar one.

The way that we know God is love is not only by the fact that God said, "I am love," but because of the evidence He has provided in revealing His love. Consider the multitude of stories found in the Bible demonstrating His patient forbearance, His mercy, His grace, and His continual provision for our planet, culminating in Christ's death on the cross as the overwhelming evidence of divine love.

God doesn't have to rely on proclamations or slogans, because He has the evidence on His side. But since Satan has no evidence, he attempts to convince people through claims and assertions.

Remember when Bill Clinton stood before the nation and proclaimed, "I did not have sexual relations with that woman"? But when Monica Lewinsky brought out her dress and it was subjected to DNA testing, the evidence revealed the truth. Satan has no truth, so he celebrates when Christians practice methods that rely on claims without evidence because it sets them up for deception.

The Lord does not want us to believe based merely on the weight of His personal assertions. Following the resurrection of Christ, two individuals walked along the road to Emmaus when a third joined them. We know the latter was Christ, but they did not recognize Him.

Discouraged by Christ's crucifixion, these disciples were unaware that He had risen. How did Christ handle the situation? He could have chosen to demonstrate His identity to them in great power and declare, "It is I, the risen Savior. Believe on Me." Instead, He led them through the evidence of the Old Testament scriptures that predicted the events in His life. It was only when they were convinced on the weight of the scriptural evidence that He revealed Himself to them.

God does not want us to believe on the basis of personal declarations and claims. Rather He desires that we believe the truth because of evidence. In the book of Isaiah God says, "Come now, let us reason together." "Though your sins are like scarlet, they shall be white as snow; though they are red as crimson, they shall be like wool" (Isa. 1:18). The process of reasoning out the evidence and discovering the truth for ourselves dispels lies from our minds and transforms us back to Christlikeness. This cannot occur just by believing declarations. To accept claims without evidence destroys reason and enfeebles the mind, turning us into unthinking shadows of others.

2. If It's Good Enough for Mom . . .

Unfortunately this is a fairly common practice in Christianity—to believe based on what someone you love or trust has said. Recently the Anglican Church changed its official belief on hell. Traditionally it had held that hell was a place of eternal fiery torment. Recently, though, the Anglican Church modified its position and now teaches that the wicked, in the end, are completely annihilated, arguing that the doctrine of eternal torment makes God into a "sadistic monster."[*]

Imagine a member of the Anglican Church raising the question of hell with someone who believes in eternal torment. If those who hold to the concept of eternal torment respond by saying, "I believe in an eternal burning hell because that's what my parents believe," would they be thinking for themselves? Would such a response reveal the use of reason or its dethronement? Or what if they said, "Well, that's what my pastor says"? Or "I've believed this my entire life; I'm not going to change now"? Such responses reveal that reason is sidelined, that those individuals have closed their minds to any further truth.

3. So Many People Can't Be Wrong

One of my favorite responses indicating that reason is not involved occurs when someone announces, "Most churches teach this. So many people can't be wrong." But those who use this argument to keep reason disengaged forget that the majority of people at the time of Noah and at the time of Christ were wrong. No, majority vote doesn't necessarily indicate truth.

4. Anger and Refusal to Ask Questions

An unfortunate but equally certain evidence that reason has been paralyzed appears when people react with anger to questions about their beliefs. Because truth can afford to be investigated, those who possess truth aren't threatened when questions arise. But positions based on error will fall apart when investigated, and so people who are unsure about the validity of their beliefs will avoid examining them whenever possible. Anger and refusal to ask questions are frequent signs that reason is inactive.

This is true even when some believe the truth, but do so because someone else has told them what to believe rather than them reasoning it out for themselves. Such individuals will experience anger when questions arise because they have never thought through the issues for themselves and don't know the evidence and rationale for why they believe what they do. Their reason is also dormant.

5. Blind Faith

When asked about something that makes no sense or for which they have no evidence, many people reply that they "just take it on faith." As we have already seen in our chapter about faith, however, true faith rests on evidence, so it never takes the position of avoiding any search for further evidence. No, only Satan's counterfeits demand acceptance without evidence, since he knows that the pursuit of evidence would destroy the false belief.

6. Satan's Greatest Achievement: Spiritualism

Satan exults when Christians promulgate methods that actually result in the slow erosion of the image of God within. Unfortunately, too many such unhealthy methods have made their way into Christian circles.

Perhaps Satan's greatest achievement within Christianity is the introduction of spiritualism. As we discovered at the end of our chapter about faith, spiritualism is the pursuit of knowledge without the investigation of evidence or the use of reason.

In certain Christian circles the deception is widespread. In fact, for many, supernatural experiences substitute for close examination of Scripture, and they base belief on volatile emotions rather than on a reasonable understanding of the truth. Nothing could be more dangerous than this combination. It is actually the complete reversal of God's hierarchy of the mind, allowing powerful feelings to serve as evidence, while paralyzing reason with the deception that the working of the Holy Spirit cannot be understood but must be accepted merely on faith.

Some circles believe that the Holy Spirit influences people to gyrate violently on the floor or laugh uncontrollably. But the Bible is unequivocal that the fruits of the Holy Spirit include "love, joy, peace, patience, kindness, goodness, faithfulness, gentleness and *self-control*" (Gal. 5:22, 23).

When the Holy Spirit has His way in our lives, we recover greater and greater self-control—we don't lose it. It is the spirit of Satan that wants to turn beings created in the image of God into brute beasts, creatures of instinct who flop around on the floor like fish, with loss of their reasoning abilities.

But because many of these experiences *feel* so good, those who have them often accept them as the leading of the Spirit of God. If only reason were reengaged and the persons involved in such activities would recall that James 1:14 reminds us that we are tempted by our feelings. If only people would value truth regardless of how it feels, then God could complete His goal of re-creating His image within. If only . . .

⋆ *The Mystery of Salvation: The Story of God's Gift. A Report by the Doctrine Commission of the Church of England* (London: Church House Publishing, 1995), p. 197.

CHAPTER 15

Coming Out of the Shadows

With large green eyes, olive skin, and brown hair, Crystal was quite stunning, and could easily be mistaken for a high fashion model. On closer inspection, however, she seemed childlike, insecure, and frightened, exuding an endearing innocence that masked an ocean of hidden hurt and pain. She seemed to communicate, without words, her longing for love and acceptance.

At age 19 Crystal stood five feet eight inches tall and weighed 103 pounds. Her gynecologist had referred her to me because of her persistent weight loss. As we discussed her situation, Crystal told me she felt "fat," and when she felt fat, she felt ugly. Therefore, she wouldn't eat because she hated feeling ugly.

Crystal reported that her childhood had been difficult because her mother had demanded perfection, and Crystal believed that she could never measure up to her mother's expectations. She reported that her mother was constantly critical. No matter how hard she tried, Crystal never experienced her mother's approval. She also recounted that her uncle had sexually molested her from the ages of 5 to 14, but she had never told anyone for fear of what they might think.

When Crystal was approximately 16 years old, she began to restrict her diet as a way to take control of her life. Eating became the focus of her interactions with her parents, often involving constant battles with her mother, who tried to force Crystal to eat more.

When the daughter wouldn't comply, her mother responded critically with such comments as "I don't care whether you eat or not. I don't care whether you live or die." Crystal felt extremely hurt and rejected by her mother, yet continued to seek her validation, approval, and acceptance.

Preoccupied with concerns about what her mother thought about her, Crystal devoted a great deal of time and energy attempting to please her. Although she realized that her mother controlled her with guilt and ridicule, Crystal was terrified by the thought of breaking free from the woman's grip. Crystal allowed her mother to make most of her decisions, and she accepted her mother's views on most topics. Not once had she openly disagreed with her mother. Although she was now little more than a shadow of her mother, inside, Crystal longed to be her own person.

During our work together Crystal continued to lose weight and dropped to 92 pounds. Her menstrual periods stopped, and she began having fainting spells. To prevent her body from experiencing multiple organ failure, she was hospitalized on three occasions. Indeed, she was literally struggling for her life.

Crystal suffered from many irrational and illogical beliefs that neared delusional proportions, such as believing that she was fat when she weighed only 92 pounds. She also assumed that because of some inadequacy within her, she had never secured her mother's approval. As a result, she constantly found fault with herself—a consequence that merely fueled the false belief that she was inadequate.

After a series of sessions I drew several conclusions about her situation. It was clear that the root of Crystal's problem lay in the dethronement and neutralization of her reason, the distortion of her conscience that constantly bombarded her with inappropriate guilt, and the adoption of a system of false beliefs encouraged by the continual domination of her negative feelings and her complete vulnerability to the opinion of others. Crystal had never learned how to balance her mind in the proper hierarchical order.

Given the severity of her illness, we had to use several medications to stabilize her biology and to enable her to receive maximal benefit from psychotherapy. The focus of therapy was to strengthen and restore her reason, purify her conscience, and establish her mental faculties as the governing agencies in her mind. It became extremely important that she learn to examine her feelings in light of truth and evidence, and then value the truth—regardless of how she felt. It was no easy task.

Crystal was able to recognize that although she considered herself "fat," she had no evidence to support such an opinion. In fact, she was finally able to acknowledge that the evidence revealed just the opposite—she was seriously underweight.

Recognition of the evidence relating to her weight did not eliminate the feeling of being fat. It did, however, allow her to realize that when she felt fat, her feelings did not stem from actually being overweight, but were connected to something else.

She came to understand that the "feeling of fatness" was the "feeling of ugliness" in disguise. She then utilized her reason to explore where the feeling of ugliness originated, and soon realized that it had its roots in her mother's constant ridicule and in her uncle's abuse. Next she began to explore the truth that her mother's "ugly" behavior revealed "ugliness" in her mother, not in Crystal. Similarly, the abuse she suffered from her uncle was itself "ugly" and disgusting, but she certainly was not.

As she began to recognize and apply the truth, healthy and accurate understandings slowly replaced the distortions and false conclusions. The truth was setting her free. As Crystal viewed the situation more clearly, she saw that others were fallible, and she began to value truth more than the opinion of others. This allowed for greater autonomy in the exercise of her will.

But Crystal's problems did not occur in isolation. As she struggled for health and autonomy, she met resistance at home. The young woman reported that her mother continued to dictate all of her actions. She had no freedom to select her own clothes, her own activities, or even her own classes in college.

After we had explored the principles of freedom, she grasped that her individuality and freedom were persistently under assault from her mother. Crystal learned that as she submitted to her mother's control, she lost respect for herself and experienced resentment toward her mother. She realized that she had become a shadow of her mother. More important, Crystal understood that if she didn't take action, she might never become her own person.

When we invited her parents to join her for family therapy, her father was willing, but her mother refused. Crystal realized the importance of learning to think for herself, and she began in the smallest way to exercise her own individuality by choosing to wear a shirt her mother had not selected for her. Her mother accused her of being rebellious and unsupportive. She told her daughter that she was a disappointment to her.

Crystal was able to recognize that her mother was the unsupportive one, so she made arrangements to move out of her parents' home and in with a friend. Her mother refused to help in any way.

When moving day arrived, her father gave her a hug, told her he loved her, and said goodbye, but her mother refused to come out of her room, not even to say goodbye. Although it caused Crystal to feel as if she were doing something terribly wrong, she was able to exercise her reason to examine the facts, which revealed that her actions were healthy and that her mother was behaving inappropriately. She saw that her mother was again trying to control her through guilt, so she chose to allow her mother the freedom to pout.

The incident confirmed that Crystal had made great progress. Although she was not pleased with how her mother was treating her, she was able to tolerate those feelings and exercise her will to choose to act on the truth, in spite of how she felt.

During the course of several months Crystal continued to practice independent thinking and to exercise her will to decide what she determined was best. As she continued to think and act for herself, her mood and weight continued to improve. Eventually she was able to sever the unhealthy connection with her mother and to accept herself for who she was, not for what her mother thought.

When we ended our therapy, Crystal weighed 117 pounds, was no longer on medications, and had enrolled in college preparing for law school. I heard from her 18 months after therapy had ended that her weight remained around 120 pounds, that she was making excellent grades in college, and that she and her mother were slowly developing a healthier relationship.

What made the difference for Crystal? Reestablishing the hierarchical balance of the faculties of her mind, learning to use her reason, clearing her conscience from distortions, removing false beliefs from her mind, learning to tolerate and examine feelings rather than accepting them as facts, and valuing truth more than the opinions of others. Crystal began implementing the law of liberty and gave her mother the freedom to think whatever she wanted without trying to change her mother's opinion. As a result, she was able to recognize and value the truth, even if her mother didn't. Having emerged out of the shadows, Crystal now stood in the fullness of her God-given individuality. She was a thinker, not a mere reflection of someone else.

This is the process that the Bible describes as growing up in Christ, as becoming a mature Christian. Mature Christians are those who have developed the ability to discern truth from the error, to think for themselves, to tolerate negative feelings, to maintain self-control, and to value truth over the opinion and approval of others. This restored unity with God is the entire focus of the Bible—it is God's plan of salvation.

Consider that *salvation* derives from the root *salve,* which means "to heal." God's plan of salvation involves taking us as sick, weak-minded, selfish beings and healing the damage in our minds, restoring the ability to think clearly, love freely, act justly, and stand solidly for what is right, and thereby transforming us from God's enemies into His friends.

CHAPTER 16

The Mind Restored

"Everything depends on the kind of God one believes in. . . .
Instead of automatically blaming the person who does not
believe in a God, we should ask first if his notion of God is
a god that ought to be believed in."—*George MacDonald.*

After I became aware of the hierarchy of the mind, I continued my research and discovered several important principles essential to achieving and maintaining mental wellness. Earlier we discussed the law of worship and learned that we actually become like the God we admire and worship. We found that misconceptions about Him result in rebellion, suffering, and pain.

The picture we hold of God is so important because it directly shapes the development of our individual characters as we incorporate into our lives the traits, principles, and methods of the God we serve. The tragic terrorist attacks on September 11, 2001, demonstrate this principle. Those who carried out the attacks believed that the murder of innocent people would please the deity they worshipped. Given this reality, I would like to share my personal belief about our origin, God's purpose in our creation, and ultimately about the God I serve.

The Origin of Evil

Long ago the universe was perfect and pure, no sound of discord existed anywhere, and all was harmony and peace. God reigned supreme, all-powerful yet equally gracious, gladly providing everything for the benefit and happiness of His intelligent creatures. He withheld nothing that could bring joy and benefit. And He enjoyed intimate communion with His intelligent creatures. One of His closest relationships was with a being called Lucifer (see Isa. 14). The Lord blessed Lucifer with every gift imaginable: great intelligence, beauty, riches, glory, authority, talent, influence, and freedom of will. Lucifer held an exalted position second only to that of God Himself and His Son.

The name Lucifer means "light bearer." We still hear echoes of his name in words such as il*lu*minate or *lu*minescence. He had the great honor of being foremost of the created beings in knowing God and then sharing his knowledge, his light, about Him throughout the universe.

Imagine yourself an angel in heaven. You've known Lucifer your entire existence and have enjoyed traveling with him and praising God alongside him. Lucifer is your commander, your counselor, your trusted friend, and your close confidant. From him you have learned many wonderful insights about God, and now he has just come from the divine presence with new and fascinating details about God—things that you've never heard before. But these characterizations are troubling, unsettling, and scary.

Lucifer reminds you of the immense power of God, and then he suggests that if any of God's intelligent creatures don't act according to His plan, He will use His power to hurt and destroy them. He implies that as long as everyone does as God intends, there is the appearance of freedom. But if anyone steps out of line and violates His law, God will use His power to punish.

What would you do? So you go to God and say, "Lucifer has suggested things about You that are very disturbing, things that are even frightening. If they are true, they would shatter my trust in You. I love You, God, but I love Lucifer, too. I don't want to choose."

God might respond, "I'm glad you love Me. And I'm glad you love Lucifer, too. Trust Me: What Lucifer is saying is untrue." Then you leave God's presence reassured. Finding Lucifer, you announce, "I just spoke with God, and He told me that what you're saying is not true."

"That's just the point," Lucifer replies. "God's lying!"

What could God do? How could He respond? Why doesn't He simply proclaim that He is telling the truth and that Lucifer is lying?

The Evidence Is on God's Side

Imagine you're the pastor of a large church. Your brother, who is the head elder, quietly and subtly circulates among the members of the congregation, asking people to put you on their prayer list because you've been embezzling money from the congregation. He hopes that those prayers will be answered, that you will repent, and that you will return the funds.

Of course, you haven't taken a cent. But your brother has sown seeds of doubt. When you discover what he is doing, how do you react? If you face the entire congregation to proclaim your innocence, will that convince everyone? No way. So what do you do? You call in an outside auditor, and line by line, ledger by ledger, as every penny gets accounted for, the truth and the evidence exonerate you and expose the liar.

What could God do? The confusion Satan had stirred up was raging through the universe. Factions began to form, the uncertainty of the angels increased, and as Lucifer's subtle distortions took hold, God said, *"Let there be light . . . Let there be a firmament . . . Let the dry land appear . . ."* As Lucifer made false declarations about the heavenly Father and His Son, God gave evidence that He is the Creator.

Humanity Was Created to Reveal the Truth About God

God didn't simply make proclamations. No! He offered evidence, revealed, demonstrable truth. The anticipation begins building in heaven as the universe sees God creating. "Did you see what God just made today? What do you think He will do tomorrow?" And the attention of the entire universe found itself drawn to our little world with keen anticipation, awaiting God's continued demonstration of the answers to Lucifer's allegations.

And on the sixth day, with the entire universe watching, God said, *"Let us make man in our image"* (Gen. 1:26). "Male and female created he them" (verse 27, KJV). As the Father, Son, and Holy Spirit come together in union and create in Their image, so man and woman would come into union and procreate in their image. And after God had made humanity, He told him to be fruitful and multiply in a perfect world without sin.

Before sin entered our world, it was God's design that Adam and Eve would have children in a perfect environment—one governed by the law of love and liberty. Why do parents have children? Do they bring them into the world to enslave, to manipulate, to exploit, or to abuse? Or do parents dedicate their time, energy, love, and resources all for the benefit of their children? How much more so in a world before sin.

Such a demonstration would have revealed to the onlooking universe the truth about how God treats His creatures: that God did not create them to exploit, enslave, abuse, or control. Instead, He constantly gives of Himself for the welfare of His creation. Can you imagine the high calling that God created humanity to fulfill? Through their caring for the planet and their nurturing of their children, humanity was to illustrate the truth about how God governs His universe! God created the human race in His image to reveal the truth about Himself!

Satan Hijacked God's Creation

Satan recognized humanity's importance. He also realized that if the universe understood the evidence humanity's creation would offer, it would expose his lies and crush his rebellion. To block God's plan, Satan returned to the same strategy that he had used in his efforts to confuse his fellow angels in heaven. This time he directed his deception at our planet and specifically at Adam and Eve.

His intention was to hijack God's creation and prevent humanity from revealing the truth about God by so damaging the human mind that it would reveal a nature completely contrary to the Creator. To accomplish this, he approached Adam and Eve and misrepresented God. He called the divine trustworthiness into question. "Did God really say in the day you eat thereof you would die? Oh, no, you won't. Look at me," the serpent declared. "I can talk because I ate of the tree. God knows if you eat from the tree you will become gods yourself, and He is trying to keep that from you" (see Gen. 3).

Sadly, following this encounter Adam and Eve—God's beautiful creation, fashioned in His image to represent the truth about Him—rebelled against their heavenly Father and became tools of Satan to further misrepresent God before the universe.

Adam's character immediately changed from one that encompassed love and self-sacrifice to a persona that included fear and selfishness. Instead of sacrificing himself to protect Eve, he blamed her and tried to excuse himself.

The onlooking universe suffered terrible confusion, wondering if Adam accurately reflected his Creator. Was Lucifer right after all? Was God selfish like Adam, unwilling to sacrifice Himself (in this case, for His creation), or would He instead sacrifice His creation to save Himself? Therefore, Jesus became the second Adam, not to pay a penalty the first Adam owed, but to finish the work the first Adam failed to accomplish—to reveal the truth about God, and to answer the questions and provide the evidence that would protect the unfallen universe and set us free from the lies that bind us.

The Sabbath Is Evidence of Our Freedom With God

After God finished creating our world in His attempt to reveal the truth about Himself, He provided one of the greatest evidences of His guarantee of individual freedom: the weekly Sabbath.

Imagine yourself again as an angel in heaven during the time that Lucifer's rebellion began. You have heard Lucifer suggest that if you step out of line, God will use His power to punish and destroy. Lucifer explains that your freedom is counterfeit because God grants apparent blessings as long as you do what He dictates. If you step out of line, though, He will get you. And then you have just witnessed God create a new world, an overwhelming display of power. More stirrings of doubt begin running through your mind. "What if Lucifer is right? What if God is displaying His immense power to intimidate, to pressure, to coerce? Is He simply flexing His muscles to scare us into conformity?"

But as you contemplate Lucifer's subtle misrepresentations, God intervenes: "Universe, you have heard the allegations of Lucifer; you have heard the testimony of the Father, the Son, and the Spirit; and you have seen the evidence just given. Now, take 24 hours aside and consider this for yourselves. I rest My case." And God created the Sabbath to further refute Satan's allegations and reveal that with God we experience real freedom of thought and choice.

The Sabbath reveals that God will never use His might to force His way. What does it say about Him that, in the context of an assault against His throne and government, He grants freedom to choose? What does it say about God that, in the context of allegations that He is untrustworthy and abusive, He creates a day to reason and to make freewill choices rather than use His power to force every knee in the universe to bow? The Sabbath provides convincing evidence that Lucifer is lying. With God, we truly are free!

Incredible God! Awesome Creator! How can you not trust a God who respects your freedom to choose?

The Truth About God

It is by understanding the truth about God that we value His character, principles, and methods of doing things, and therefore trust Him. Our trust rests on the revelation of evidence that He has given to demonstrate His trustworthiness. This reestablished trust expels fear from our hearts, and we begin again to operate from motives of love rather than selfishness, fear, and guilt.

Our reason is ennobled, our conscience cleansed, our will is strengthened, and we freely choose to practice God's methods of love and liberty. It's only natural that we become more and more like Him. Our self-governance, dignity, and God-given nobility of character are restored. We operate on the principles of love, freedom, truth, and openness—ever advancing, ever maturing, ever achieving victory after victory as we are changed from God's enemies into His friends, looking forward to the day that we shall meet Him face to face.

∞

I don't know where my patient from the preface is now. I don't know how She is doing. Nor do I know whether She is alive or has succeeded in ending Her own life. But if She is alive, if She is still hurting, if She is still struggling to find answers—answers that I couldn't provide those many years ago—I hope that this book finds Her and that, in it, She will find answers to heal Her pain and bring peace to Her mind.

I am praying for Her.